For Bob Albrook

George S. Reeves
June 10,

A MAN FROM
SOUTH DAKOTA

A MAN FROM
SOUTH DAKOTA

BY

GEORGE S. REEVES

E. P. DUTTON & COMPANY, INC.
NEW YORK, 1950

To

ROY *and* MABEL COWDEN

CONTENTS

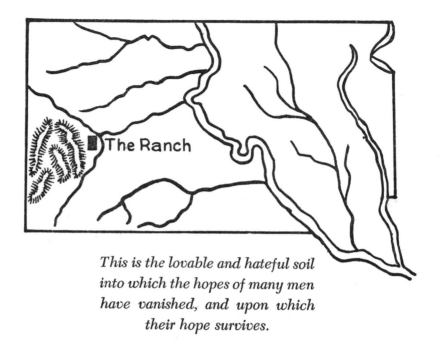

*This is the lovable and hateful soil
into which the hopes of many men
have vanished, and upon which
their hope survives.*

A MAN FROM
SOUTH DAKOTA

Chapter I

THE OTHER SIDE OF ZERO

In 1936, on the very bottom of the Dust Bowl years, I heard a rancher say, "Since I came to this goddam country in 1880, there's only been two good years — 1916, and Next Year." Though some people left in '36, he didn't. And in '46 I saw him driving a big, new car. But he's cursing Dakota again this year. It's that kind of country.

None of this shows on the map. South Dakota has the kind of boundaries that a sixth-grade geography student can draw with a ruler, four inches for four hundred miles. The capital is in the center, and so, for that matter, is the center of North America. On paper, almost everything about it seems to come out even.

It is only in the southeast corner that the map gives a hint of the kind of forces that surge beneath it. There the Sioux River and the Missouri break out of the state, carrying the boundary with them in a shifting line to the point of their confluence, and it takes more than a geographer's surveying instrument to hold that boundary intact, for the Missouri in flood can dig a new channel for itself in the space of a few hours, and several square miles of bottomland can change statehood overnight. Breakwaters have to be kept in constant readiness at the danger points, or the mapping of four states would have to be edited annually, like a calendar. The Missouri is that kind of river.

Within the state, this unruly stream continues to bound and to divide. It draws a deep line of geological difference between the east and the west half of the state. The east was engulfed by the Ice Sheet, the river flowed around its edge, and the west half was never touched by glaciation. Approaching from the east the traveler can cross the political boundary unaware of its existence, and there is no point at which the rich alluvial plains of Minnesota and Iowa visibly become South Dakota.

But as the plain spreads westward, a slow turbulence gathers beneath it, there is a gain in altitude, and the air has a clearer, cleaner quality. Now and then a stream cross-cuts a blue shale bank to leave a dark scar which hints of thinner soil. Where the Missouri cuts through this shale, there is no longer any doubt that untamed rock lies close beneath the surface. Beyond the muddy, swift-flowing stream the land resumes its slow climb through a region of rolling, grassy hills. A hundred miles from the river, these hills crest sharply into the barren peaks known as the Bad Lands, only to regain the grassy covering beyond. All told the traveler must traverse two hundred miles of treeless land before he raises the first glimpse of black timbered slopes that mark the Black Hills, which are the center and the shore of this tumbled prairie surf.

The archaeologist would search this region in vain for any monuments or relics of civilized antiquity, and the historian poring over dusty tomes would find no record of an ancient past. For, in the human sense, it has no ancient past; and — because it was screened from early explorers by its bleak ring of grassy hills — it has little recent past.

During the long blank centuries when other parts of the world echoed to the babel of human voices, and Indian tribes already spoke their guttural tongues on the North American Continent, there were few voices here. The cold streams of the Black Hills laved no thirsty human throats. The hailstorms that battered wide pathways of destruction across the prairie swales threatened no human hopes. The warm chinook winds which poured down off the mountains, though they held the Ice Sheet at bay, invited no Arctic tribes. The hills were here, the fish and the game, the spruce and the pine, but no one knew or cared. The Black Hills were an uncharted island of trees in an ocean of grass.

In every direction, the grass covered the earth with a tough hide of sod that repelled seedling trees and blessed the buffalo. The buffalo filled the prairie vistas from sky line to sky line with dense shaggy hordes of powerful and short-tempered animals — to a number of 70,000,000 head some guessers say.

The ancestors of the Sioux, fumbling their way eastward from the Bering Sea, were not tempted by this menacing, barren prairie. It offered few trees for concealment, no

15

cliffs such as the Cliff Dwellers found in the Southwest, few streams navigable even by canoe. The horse was still in Europe, the bow and arrow still in Asia, and buffalo country was no place for a man afoot. These spear-bearing prowlers passed silently by, moving eastward into the safer shelter of the timbered Mississippi Valley.

But the Sioux were defeated in the East. Harried and decimated by the Iroquois, they retreated until their backs were against the open prairie, and when they reached it this time, the horse had appeared upon it.

Cortez had brought horses to the continent in the sixteenth century. Some had escaped riderless in battle, and as the long decades passed, and new generations of young stallions jealously herded their harems of mares farther and farther away from the attention of other stallions, they had populated the grasslands with uncounted thousands of slim-barreled and fleet saddle stock.

The Sioux discovered their use. From that time on the Sioux suffered no more defeats. Mounted, they lived upon buffalo meat, and they fought their enemies on better than even terms.

Thus began a vigorous and cruel domination of the northern Great Plains. The Sioux disliked visitors of any kind, and among the first visitors to fall victim to their dislike was South Dakota's first author.

Working with a penknife on both sides of a small slab of sandstone, he wrote, "Came to these hills in 1833, seven of us, De Lacompt, Ezra Kind, G. W. Wood, F. Brown,

R. Kent, Wm. King, Indian Crow. All ded but me Ezra Kind. Killed by Inds beyond the high hill. Got our gold June 1834. Got all of the gold we could carry. Our ponys all got by the Indians. I have lost my gun and nothing to eat and Indians hunting me."

He mailed his manuscript under a rock ledge on Lookout Mountain, where it lay, unpublished, till 1887. What his death was can only be guessed. One method of the Sioux was to stake a victim on the ground and keep a fire burning on his stomach until he was dead.

Ezra Kind's failure to escape cost the Black Hills 42 years of history. Fifteen years after his death, gold was discovered in California, and in Montana thirty years later. It was not until 1876 that men poured into Deadwood Gulch, to rediscover Ezra's find, to loot it of seven million dollars, and to locate the billion-dollar mother lode from which it had come. When Ezra's memorandum was uncovered in 1887, the news came so late that for years many thought it was a fake, like the Cardiff giant.

Long after the gold discovery, the Black Hills remained an isolated island of human settlement completely surrounded by buffalo country, and in the winter of '82-'83 even the buffalo deserted the surrounding grasslands. That winter the Ice Sheet came back for a return engagement, and the Arctic Circle reached down as far as the Texas Panhandle to reclaim some of its ancient domain. Drifts a hundred feet in depth clung to the mountain slopes above Lead City and Deadwood Gulch, and the grass of the prairies was triple-locked in ice, as Arctic cold and snow blanketed the entire region from Canada to Mexico.

For centuries the buffalo had trusted the winter pasture on these plains. The grass, green in spring, cured in autumn and retained its richness throughout the winter. The tides of buffalo had ebbed and flowed northward and southward with the snow line, to Oklahoma and Texas in the winter and to Canada in the spring. Now they were betrayed. More deadly than the guns of the buffalo hunters, far more complete than any destruction at human hands, ice and snow stamped them out in one deadly blow.

When spring came no buffalo moved upon the Great Plains. Men on its western border thought the herds had changed their pathway and had passed to the eastward. Men on the eastern fringe of the prairie-plowland thought the buffalo had passed to the westward. The buffalo had passed nowhere. They were dead.

When my father crossed the Missouri River in a caboose in 1890, he saw grass waving in unbroken domination from sky line to sky line. The buffalo were gone, and nothing had replaced them. Save for an occasional band of Indian ponies fleeing from the train which bore him westward, the land was untenanted, unplowed, running endlessly to waste. My father was an orderly man and he thought this land should be useful for something.

He had been born on a Kentucky hill farm, within sight of the Blue Grass and its sleek horses. But there were no horses on his father's farm — there wasn't enough land.

18

There was only a hoe for the tobacco fields and a mule to ride to town. There was also a stepmother who begrudged the small coins his father paid him for hoeing tobacco.

The ancestors of the Sioux, looking eastward from Asia, had seen a land populous with game across the Bering Sea; Ezra Kind had seen escape from dawn-to-dark work in the fur barges on the St. Louis water front; but my father heard the haunting promise of freedom in the long wail of a locomotive whistle. He followed it over the windowsill one night at the age of twelve, and hoed tobacco no more.

By the time he came to South Dakota he had long since caught up with the locomotive whistle. He had done a stint in Oklahoma Territory as a telegraph operator and he was "deadheading through" to a promotion in Deadwood Gulch. But as the broad untenanted square miles flowed slowly past the window of the caboose, his mind was not on the train whistle from which the Indian ponies fled. It was on the land.

My mother was in the Black Hills ahead of him, living with her father and mother and my uncle in the rooms over the hardware store. Though she had never been on the ocean, seagoing vessels had brought her there.

Her father, as a lad, had been apprenticed to a cabinet-maker in Plymouth, England. The terms of his apprenticeship were harsh and its future cramped, so, to gain better, he risked worse. He came to America, in time to carry

19

a musket in the Civil War. Afterward he built oil tanks in the Pennsylvania oil field, salt tanks in the Michigan salt fields, and houses in Fremont, Nebraska, believing that Fremont would become the city which Omaha eventually became. The trade of carpentry had dogged him grimly that far. But in the midst of a grasshopper plague which destroyed his faith in Fremont, gold was discovered in the Black Hills.

He bought a bull team and two wagonloads of flour, and with his carpenter tools in the wagon with him, he arrived in Deadwood Gulch at just the right time to sell the flour for fifty dollars a sack. He also sold the carpenter tools and went back for two wagonloads of them. So he put his name on a hardware store on Main Street in Lead City, Dakota Territory, and carpentry saw him no more.

When mining ventures had placed my grandfather beyond the reach of counter-jumping, and my father had married my mother, they pooled a common interest in land. In 1903, my father and grandfather bought two and a half square miles of prairie, and the name they put up on the gate was Salmon & Reeves.

So, thanks to sailing vessels, a caboose, a bull team, and the timely death of Ezra Kind, I owned a ranch two years before I was born, and one night in March of 1905, I also entered South Dakota through a boundary of pain.

Chapter II

FROM THE MOUTHS OF BABES

In June of 1926, when I was twenty-one, and the Salmon & Reeves coalition was about to produce its first Bachelor of Arts, I was summoned into the office of the head of the Rhetoric Department. I found the professor seated in an office whose walls were lined with books, and as I entered, the books seemed to bristle like the guns of a fortress, for my final examinations were still in the mill and I was afraid that I had been summoned because my bachelor's degree had been gored by someone's red pencil. But it soon developed that the professor wanted to ask advice of someone from South Dakota.

There was a man in his department, he said, who was looking for a piece of farm land on which to retire from teaching. The professor had in his own youth visited the western part of my state and had seen a great deal of very rich land which apparently was not being used for anything but grazing. Some of this land had been settled by now, he supposed, but he had heard that since the collapse of the war boom land values were quite low, and he had immediately thought of western South Dakota as an ideal situation for his friend. What did I think of the possibility of acquiring land out there at a reasonable figure, now, when the price was low, rather than waiting for actual retirement?

The question reversed our roles. Though the professor had gray whiskers, and mine were still on a biweekly basis; and though it seemed probable that he had read every book in the place, it was plain that when it came to knowing anything about South Dakota land, he was an ignoramus and a dumbbell. People don't retire to South Dakota land, they retire from it.

I was only twenty-one, but I knew that much. For, in the ten years since my father's death, I had been living in intimate contact with Dakota land, and for the past seven years I had been living with my aunt and uncle on the ranch. What I knew now at twenty-one, they hadn't known at forty-five when they had tried to retire to it.

They had made their decision in the spring of 1919, when the price of beef was high, when wheat promised to go higher, and when it seemed most likely that any acreage planted to wheat would inevitably grow into money. The renter who had been on the place for some years now had a "big car." We still drove a flivver.

Aunt Ida saw the risk and was hesitant, but Uncle Harry saw escape from the deadly monotony of working for a mining company, seven days a week until he retired. He wanted to retire now, while wheat was high and he had some vigor left with which to grow it.

The plan slowly unfolded among the bread crumbs on the dining-room tablecloth. A new Fordson tractor and plows would cost twelve hundred dollars. Wheat could be planted, beef cows bought and calved. Out of the wheat and the cattle would come the money to buy some things they both wanted.

"It will take every cent we've saved," Aunt Ida said, "but it will get you out of that deadly grind at the Plant."

"You have to spend money to make money," Uncle Harry said. "One good year and we'll have it all back with profit to spare."

Though I was only fourteen, I was Uncle Harry's staunch ally. For I had spent three summers with the renter's boys on the ranch and none of the summers had been long enough. To my young eyes (and to eyes far older than mine) it was a magnificent toy. When I rode a pony across the upland pasture at a ringing trot, the words "the West" came to life. The mountains climbed to the westward in long strides, the yucca grew upon the barren hills, and the prairie rolled to the sky line just as it had in the old free days when men carried six-shooters and the country was wild. The saddle horse under me, the .22 rifle in the saddle holster, the very coyotes which howled at night, made me content with the word "rancher." In the evening the sunset stained the sky behind the mountains with the colors of cathedral glass, and the Big Dipper framed the Butte as though it had been made to fit. It seemed to me very clever of God to have arranged the stars in the firmament to fit the Butte in such a graceful way.

But during the winter of our decision, my attention was

temporarily distracted from this matter of becoming a rancher by another matter of equal moment. I was making the discovery that sometimes a Westerner has to buckle on his guns and ride off into the desert alone.

A girl moved to town that winter who wore a lemon-colored greatcoat that I could see for blocks. At school she sat in a seat two rows removed from mine. My glance turned easily in that direction, but if her eyes met mine, my own eyeballs fairly clicked in making their escape. On the street I was conscious of that lemon-colored coat until it disappeared into a house, when I turned discontentedly to less exhilarating sights. It was with mingled exaltation and contentment that one Sunday I saw the coat in a pew across the aisle in church.

My attendance that day was strictly due to the fact that it was the last Sunday in the month. Once a month my aunt insisted that I stay to church after Sunday school. This was the last available Sunday. It had been my firm intention to forget that this was the last Sunday in the month, and escape before my Aunt's arrival. But she had been vigilant, and I had lost the tug of war on the church stoop.

Now, I reaped a rich reward. A strange contentment filled me that this girl should see me piously staying to church. Fixing upon the minister an intent and studious stare, I prepared to impress the young lady with my sanctity. The role proved to be my undoing, for out of the contentment that I found in her presence, I suddenly dis-

24

covered that the sounds which issued from pulpit and organ were very moving sounds indeed. When the organ boomed the Doxology, I was stirred. When the minister talked, I listened. But all the while I was acutely conscious of the girl who sat across the aisle.

My knowledge of these matters was not of the best. Among my literary authorities on the subject of love was Gene Stratton Porter's *The Harvester*, in which the characters addressed one another as "Oh Man!" and "Oh Woman!" My idea of a heroine was an elegant creature, easily wounded, apt to take offense at the slightest breach of etiquette, scrupulously moral, translucently pale, and utterly implacably perfect. Where in Heaven or Hell the authors of that day acquired their female characters it would be hard to say, but I was stuck with them. Such a creature, I felt sure, was sitting across the aisle.

Perfection such as hers, I felt, could only be approached by perfection. I diligently coveted this state.

The man in the pulpit was talking about perfection. Christ, he said, was the example of the perfect man. The minister urged all and sundry within the sound of his voice to imitate Christ. Go to the New Testament, he said, read it every night, if you would learn how to be perfect.

What I found in the New Testament did not seem to care much about my winning the girl across the aisle. In fact it stated in reasonably plain language that a man's chances in the hereafter would be a lot better if he avoided the sex altogether.

25

A MAN FROM SOUTH DAKOTA

A more practical approach to my predicament several times occurred to me, but to speak to this wonderful creature directly in plain English was a liberty my vocal chords refused to permit me. Two Sundays in a row she departed up the aisle, unpropositioned. On the third Sunday she walked off on the arm of a less thoroughly documented competitor, to my utter spiritual chagrin.

My acquaintance with books indicated that two possible courses were open to me. I could go into a monastery and live thenceforth under a vow of silence, or I could buckle on my guns and ride off into the desert alone. The move to the ranch canceled both alternatives. The imaginary world of books faded abruptly when I crossed the line fence. The ranch wasn't a desert, rain fell there too frequently; and the ranch wasn't wholly a ranch, it was partly a farm. Instead of riding a horse, I found myself on the seat of the new tractor, and very glad I was to be there. I found that there was a fascination in the purring motor and in the curling wake of sod that flowed from the plow. The soil was black and rich, and contrasted beautifully with the unplowed green. As one moved up and down the field, up and down, up and down, progress was measurable to the eye in the width of the strip of black. Somewhere, on one of those rounds, I plowed the girl under, and most of my spiritual chagrin.

But I had to fight with my uncle for possession of the tractor seat. He also had something to plow under — the memory of monotony.

FROM THE MOUTHS OF BABES

Every day for twelve years he had walked down the hill toward the Slimes Plant, carrying a lunch pail. Crossing Red Creek, he had climbed the long flight of wooden stairs to the Press Floor and walked down the seemingly endless row of cast-iron presses which dominated the plant. In the dim reaches an illuminated clock marked the stairway to the Change Room. There he donned overalls and took over where the other Press Boss had left off. For eight hours he lolled before a desk which held a few test tubes, a stop watch, and a sheet of paper on which he marked columns of figures. Overhead, a pump, — making a "change" on a press, — clanked and churned. Beneath the iron monsters slime-laden water gushed in a constant flow. The place was redolent of cyanide, damp with the splashing of water. It was my uncle's task to watch water run down hill, and deflect it at proper intervals.

In this monotony there was safety and financial security. The gold that came from the far end of the process paid him in gold pieces twice a month. In addition it paid the dividends on his Homestake stock and on that my father had left me. He had only to watch a clock eight hours, and as surely as the coming of the dawn, these moneys would happen. For twelve years, with unfailing regularity, they had happened.

But the bread and butter they provided was a limited diet for the son of a man who had declined to accept the future on similar terms in England. For a number of years Uncle Harry had taken the curse off this unleavened future

by playing with a dangerous toy. On his way home from
work it was his custom to stop in a saloon and drop a
dollar on the roulette wheel. If it won he stayed and played.
If it lost, he bought chances on a punchboard and came
home with a box of candy.

The ranch was a bigger punchboard, and the man on the
tractor a bigger gambler.

But the ranch in the summer of 1919 looked like a
roulette wheel when it is thinly played, or a punchboard
when all the numbers are punched out. After a heavy snow
in May, which seemed to promise a third abundant year in a
row, there was no more rain. The light was harsh, the sunlight uninterrupted, and the cracked earth was much too
visible where wheat and grass should have hidden it from
view. The first cutting of alfalfa had promised to be lush
and bountiful because of the snow, but a late frost had
cut it down, and the second cutting began to bloom long
before it was high enough to mow.

The wheat that we had planted on old alfalfa ground
withered before it started to head and we cut it for hay.
But the sod wheat was a thinner stand and still hung on,
and the sod corn was a healthy green. On the Fourth of
July three inches of rain rescued the early wheat from
burning and worked wonders in the sod corn. Things were
looking up, we thought.

Every day, when Uncle Harry and I were working
together around the barns and corrals, "fixing up the

place," he would drop his tools, straighten up and say, "Let's go out and look at the wheat."

Then we would crank the Ford and drive out to pore over our chances of having a Buick.

The beef cows had calved in April and one day when we were riding through them, he made a remark that at the time didn't mean much to me. We were on the high hill. Below us the fields were spread out in squares. The cattle, bunched up in the shade of a near-by plum thicket, were a solid red contrasting with the green of grass and trees. "This grazing land is Single O and Double O," Uncle Harry said. "The way the crop looks, I'm glad we've got some splitters on the Green. I think I'll take a flyer in chickens too, and milk some more cows."

Milking ten cows was a job that got me up at 4:30 to bring the stock in from the pasture, and kept us both on the milk stools for more than an hour. We then had to separate the milk and feed the skim milk to ten calves. Then we rounded up the horses, curried, harnessed, and got to the hayfield by nine or ten o'clock. The cows interrupted our work but they made steady money happen at regular intervals while we were waiting for the big bets to pay off.

Every day big thunderbusters, piled high like statues of dancers carved in white marble, loomed above the line of the Black Hills to the west and promised rain. But rain came only now and then, in thin showers that merely settled the dust. The showers helped fill the kernels of the early wheat and kept the sod corn green, but they never gave us the feeling that our crops were safe.

At length we assembled the binder which had been taken apart and stored in the garage, and, hitching three horses on it, pulled it out to the wheat and let it into gear. An amazing thing happened. The reel, intended to push the heads over onto the canvases, whirled instead like a millrace, batting heads forty feet behind the canvas. Obviously this was not right.

We pored over the machine, neither of us knowing anything about it. We stabbed blindly at the problem, changing any adjustment that was susceptible to change. The reel still shot heads backward like a Gatling gun. At length we got in the Ford and went after a neighbor.

The neighbor got in the seat, clucked to the horses, and fired another volley of heads. He stopped the horses, removed a cogwheel, turned it around, put it back on and got back in the seat.

"Now I try him," he said. "I think he will work."

He clucked to the horses. Grain fell before the sickle, was pushed over onto the canvas by the reel, and was carried up into the intestines of the machine. It collected there against a mysterious arrangement of iron castings, then suddenly disgorged a bundle, neatly tied with twine. When a sufficient number of bundles had accumulated on the bundle carrier, the driver heaved mightily with his foot, and dropped them expertly to the ground.

Our neighbor stopped the team, examined the tauntness of the twine on the bundles, and said, "Now he is working all right — you just got a cogwheel on wrong."

When he had departed, Uncle Harry and I maneuvered craftily for the position on the binder seat. Uncle Harry won it, and proceeded to achieve innumerable bundles without further mishap. I followed behind, picking them up, setting them in shocks as I had learned to do in 1916.

The sun grew hot, the perimeter of the field carried me far from my water jug. The bundles scratched my arms, sharp straw penetrated my lingerie at the belt and stabbed me continuously in various places.

Uncle Harry stopped the binder beside me. "You aren't cleaning up that loose straw good enough," he said. "Wheat is three dollars a bushel, and every head is worth money."

"I'll drive the binder and you shock," I offered hopefully.

"No," he said. "You don't understand this machine, and you might as well learn your job right as to learn it wrong. Do that shocking right, and after a while I'll give you a lesson in driving the binder."

A week later we had the field cut and in the shock. The heads were short but they were filled with plump kernels. We invited estimates from neighbors who passed by. Opinions varied from five bushels to the acre to twenty-five. Naturally we preferred the estimates in the higher brackets.

It was a long wait. There was only one threshing machine in the neighborhood, and it wouldn't reach us till late fall, so we had to put the bundles in the stack. Once stacked they had to go through the "sweat" and while in this stage threshing was impossible. The fact that we had stacked it committed us to a wait of six weeks, beyond the time when school would start.

I faced school with a new dread. I was entering my second year of high school in a new town and in a larger school. Rapid City was too far from the ranch for me to come home at night and get back the next morning, so I was going to board in town through the week.

During the summer I had become something I had never been before — a country jake. I felt this rather keenly. Against the high collar of my white shirt my sunburned face looked flushed and strangled. My suit coat bit me in the shoulders and my knee pants were, to my way of thinking, a little too short and a little too tight. I ventured up the inclined walk that led to the high-school building feeling that I moved in the spotlight of the world's attention.

But once within the building I began to lose a little of the sense of my own conspicuousness. In a line waiting for a locker key, in another line waiting for my books, I was one of many. After all, school was only school, and after a summer of hard physical labor the short hours and the absence of unwelcome chores began to take on an appeal of their own. It was easier to draw an orderly circle with a compass than to ride one with a horse looking for a cow. It was easier to draw a straight line with a ruler than to plow one with a tractor, up hill and down. Plane geometry was a far more orderly game than ranch geometry.

When, on my first week end home, the threshing rig arrived and began to swallow bundles from the stack a little faster than I could pitch them comfortably, when the machine ground on long after I was tired, and when the tallying device on the machine added up our score at five bushels to the acre, I got my first inkling that a white-collar occupation might have its advantages.

"Well," said Uncle Harry, when the tally was in, "five bushels ain't bad at three dollars a bushel, but it's a hell of a long ways from buying a Buick. We'll just have to crank this Lizzie for another year. I ain't going to sell those cattle because they're going up in price, and I ain't going to sell the corn because it's worth more fed to the cattle as fodder. Next week when you come home, we'll start cutting it."

A week later we probed the mysteries of the corn binder and finally succeeded in getting a bundle out of it. Uncle Harry hired a man, and when I returned again for the week end, the corn was in the shock.

Shortly after frost, the clouds which had been so stingy since May, suddenly became generous. Snow fell, followed by more snow. It all thawed at once, and turned to mud. Then more snow fell, and turned to mud. The clutch bands on the Ford began to clatter and had to be replaced. One week end I didn't get back to school until Wednesday, and not long afterward a blizzard and intense cold kept me ranch-bound for more than a week. My report card bore the notation, "An excellent student, but absent a great deal."

I wasn't playing hooky. School would have been a welcome relief from the tasks I faced. I was learning to hate the job of thrusting cold bits into the mouths of reluctant horses, driving long miles to the stacks, tearing hay out of them in a bitter wind. I learned to hate the task of chopping corn fodder from its ice-welded grip upon the earth, and hauling it to bawling beef cattle. Latin and English and Geometry and History taught in warm school-rooms, were far more attractive than this endless struggle with hostile weather. When a chill wind was pouring into the corrals from the south, and the beef cattle shivered at the water tank, and the milk cows preferred to stay in the barn without water rather than face the wind, I was homesick for the halls of learning.

The spring saw the countryside bogged down in bottom-less mud. Using the car on the unimproved roads was out of the question, and it required at least four hours for a team and wagon to slug through that slippery clay and reach town.

Yet, with that facility for change which Dakota seemed always to possess, four days of sunshine made the fields dusty on the surface, and Uncle Harry wasted no time in discing in another heavy planting of wheat. No sooner had he finished than the rains set in again. For weeks they never stopped. All the streams were in flood, some of the houses in town were under water.

When I came home from school in June, and looked down upon the land from the hill where the road entered our line fence, I saw grass cover the vista from sky line to sky line. The ranch was knee-deep in green. Here was the land that could support seventy million buffalo, with grass left over for the grouse and quail and plover and curlews to nest in and raise their young.

As the season advanced, the purple squares of alfalfa, the yellow of sweet clover, the deep green of the wheat, urged us to hasten. Our situation of the summer before was reversed. Now plenty was pressing upon us, and the problem was to wrest it undamaged from the frequent downpours of rain.

We drove our mowers into hayfields that hid horses to the shoulders. In air heavily laden with the perfume of alfalfa, dense with swarms of grass-bred mosquitoes, we tumbled the hay in a heavy swath, raked it and then tried to get it in the stack, only to be rained out of the field when the hay was still in the shock. Some of the shocks we turned over as many as three times to dry, and finally abandoned. Stacking, as usual, was hampered by the uncertainties of the equine temperament. Twice the haystacker was wrecked again as the stacker team, goaded by flies, lunged too far and too fast. A horse would fall over the sweep tongue and break it to splinters. A team ran away with the rake and wrapped it around a cottonwood tree.

We finally finished ten stacks of hay. With enough help, and good machinery we could have put up forty.

The wheat harvest put an end to our haying. Binding was hastened by the fact that, hidden deep in the chin-high jungle of stalks, tiny flecks of rust were at work. Neighbors told us that the wheat had rusted because of the damp weather. Others said it had rusted because of spores that came from the barberry bush. But all were agreed that the wheat would have to be cut at once and permitted to ripen as much as it ever would ripen — in the shock.

The harvest of a year before was child's play compared to this one. The constant heavy flow of straw upon the canvases made the binder pull heavy. Insects, dampness, and heat sapped the strength of the teams. In two hours a team would wear out. Some days we changed teams as many as three times. As we worked, a cloud of rust obscured the binder, and the stubble behind it was almost a blood-red. Shocking was a task as discouraging as working on a rock pile is to a member of a chain gang. A stoop for every bundle, a shock for every bundle dump, and a hundred acres to cover. We hired two men, and at length saw the last of the bundles in the stack. There were eighteen big stacks in all. The field looked like an Indian settlement.

We threshed three days with a big rig and binned a nine-bushel yield of shriveled wheat. The mill buyer looked at the kernels and shook his head. "We can't use it," he said. "It won't make flour."

"To hell with you, then," said my uncle, "my chickens

can use it. Shriveled wheat is good enough for them."

"We don't sell chickens," the buyer said sourly, "we sell flour."

The hired help and the twine bill had cut into our bank account, taxes were overdue, and there was no wheat check, Uncle Harry decided to unload all of his calves and his yearlings. He went off to market with them to get some money.

But here, too, something had shriveled. From a high of eighteen cents a pound the fall before, cattle had dropped to five cents. Uncle Harry came home with a check for seven hundred and eighty-five dollars. He put it in the bank and wrote a check to pay the taxes. The first check cleared but the second didn't — the bank had closed its doors.

Uncle Harry and Aunt Ida never fully recovered from these accumulated disappointments. They made a living from their chickens and milk cows, but the Buick was dead and the hours they worked were not my idea of retirement. It was highly probable that, at the very moment I sat in the professor's book-lined office, Aunt Ida was cleaning the hen roosts with a hoe, and Uncle Harry was cleaning out the cow barn.

I didn't know who the professor's friend was, or how much he knew about farming, but I doubted very much that he knew anything about South Dakota farming and my answer was emphatic.

"My God, no!" I said. "He'll lose his shirt, unless he has a lot of money to buy livestock and machinery. That country

is no place for a small-scale operator. You have to have a
lot of land, and a lot of money to work it right. He'd better
go somewhere else to retire."

The professor was surprised by my vehemence, and I
continued in a milder tone, describing a hailstorm, a blizzard and a drought. By the time I had finished he was
apparently convinced.

Then, with the air of one who wishes to return a back-
scratching with a back-scratching, he said, "What are *you*
going to do after graduation?"

I was embarrassed, for, in the light of the advice I had
just given, my reply was bound to smack of conceit. I didn't
know why I thought I could do what my uncle and aunt
had failed to do, unless it was because they were born of
an older generation and were therefore fools, while I was
modern and had learned to Reason. But I was convinced,
and over their strenuous objections, I was going back to
do it.

"I'm going back to the ranch and buy some sheep," I
said. "I can make a better living that way than working on
a newspaper."

The professor was mildly surprised.

"You have a ranch of your own?" he asked.

"A two-thirds interest in one," I replied. "I was twenty-
one three months ago and it's mine now."

"Perhaps you would have done better to go to an agricultural school?" he suggested.

"No," I answered, "you can't learn much about South

38

Dakota ranching by going to school. The books don't fit it. The only way to learn anything about it is by being there. I've been there seven years and I know *that* much about it."

"What did you major in here?" he asked.

"Journalism," I replied since it would have been hard to explain in a single sentence that for four years I had simultaneously been the victim of three major intentions, only one of which was Journalism.

The conflict had begun in my high-school years. From the time that an English teacher told me that I had a future as an essayist, it had been my intention to become an author. Any feeling that I had for newswriting was superimposed upon that, the theory being that newswriting was the key to Irvin S. Cobbhood. I hadn't yet decided to be a Shakespeare, that came later; *The Saturday Evening Post* was my target, and journalism was to be the string to my bow.

But my aunt wanted me to study medicine. She said that my father had talked a great deal about my becoming a doctor. All through those years when he was sick and his doctor bills were high, she said, he had refused to cut into his savings because he wanted to leave money for me to study medicine.

I could see my obligation, and I could see that a doctor could acquire a great deal of firsthand story material. Perhaps I would decide to become a doctor.

Uncle Harry tacitly agreed that I should study medicine, and he admired the grades on my themes in Senior English, but now and then he would look off toward the Butte and say, "This is a good piece of land you've got here, George. When I'm dead it'll all belong to you. Don't ever let anybody talk you out of it."

"I don't intend to," I said.

"Maybe *you* can do something with it when you come of age," he went on. "I'm too old, and it takes money to make money. Last year we let three hundred tons of hay slip through our fingers because we didn't have the outfit to put it up. Maybe, when you get to be a doctor, you'll want this place. You'd better hang onto it, boy. It's better than working for a company, better by a damned sight."

My intentions as a high-school graduate, therefore, were something of a Gordian knot. I was going to be a doctor who would write novels and who would somehow find the time to operate a ranch. When it came time to choose a school in the fall the doctor was uppermost, and it was decided that for the first year I might as well attend a school near home, where premedical studies were to be had (though writing courses were not), and from which I could come home over the week ends to help with the ranch work.

What happened to my thinking during this first year of college had been in the making for some time. I had remained a voracious reader, both in school and out, and had begun to discern that much of what I read was vaguely contradictory. While it was quite obvious that Adam wasn't the first man that ever was invented, Moses had most certainly parted the waters of the Red Sea, and though water was H_2O and wine was CH_3OH, water had most certainly been turned into wine by a miracle. Something was wrong somewhere, but probably in my understanding, for I had never found it possible to doubt a printed word. Unexpectedly, I now found it possible to do so.

The geology professor was a small man with keen gray eyes, and a supply of dry humor. In his hand, on the first day, he held an apple.

"I have here an apple," he said. "I picked it this morning off the Tree of Knowledge."

There was a laugh. When it had subsided he said, "Better not quote me on that. I've been accused of producing atheists in this class, and I wouldn't want to be misunderstood. My job is to present scientific truth. What you make of it is your own business."

He walked over to the window and adjusted the shade. Then he came back to his desk and held the apple in the palm of his hand.

"To begin with," he said, "we'll say that this is the earth. The wrinkles on the skin are mountains. This worm blister is Mount Everest. The earth grew to be what it is now, just as this apple grew, imperceptibly, changing a little at a time. In this class we will try to reconstruct what the earth once was, and the forces by which it became what it is today."

Deftly he cut the apple into segments, allowing one segment to project, depressing those on either side of it.

41

"These projecting segments are continental masses," he said. "The lower ones are ocean deeps. Probably the continents have always been continents and the oceans have always been oceans. Perpetually the snows and winds and rain are carving at these high masses, the rivers are pouring them into the ocean deeps. From the concentration of the salt in the ocean we can compute its age at about three hundred and fifty million years."

I had always thought that the ocean had been made a short time before the arrival of Moses, and that the eating of an apple had mysteriously brought tragedy upon the world. I now saw that the contradictions of which I had been aware were not in my mind, but in the printed word, that somebody was a liar and that it wasn't the man who had measured the amount of salt in the ocean. That week end when I went home to the ranch, I looked at the Butte and found that it had aged. The stars of the Big Dipper pricked tiny holes in an empty sky, and life was a shorter ride than I had thought.

But I soon found that there was an exhilaration in wielding the new weapon of doubt. Most of my immediate circle of friends also possessed it, and we had long discussions in which we laid about us vigorously, knocking old superstitions off their pedestals and having a very good time.

It was only when I was alone with the Butte that I thought about the other side of it, and here I also came to some conclusions. If there were no one to watch the sparrow's fall, the answer then was not to be a sparrow, but an eagle. An eagle could achieve a sort of triumph over this cruel universe by looking down upon it and seeing and understanding it all; there would even be a sort of triumph over his own death in the act of its recognition. A dead eagle could possess a dignity that a sparrow lacked. Shakespeare, after three hundred years, still had dignity. So, in a lesser degree, had Ezra Kind. It seemed to me that an author could beat this game, if he were good enough.

During the summer vacation I made it clear to my aunt and uncle that I wanted to go to a school where courses in journalism were to be had, and that fall I landed on the Michigan campus thirteen hundred miles from home with a *Roget's Thesaurus* and a checkbook that had cost me nothing in shoveling coal into engines or husking corn. The *Thesaurus* was my idea, but the checkbook was my father's, and Michigan also had a good medical school. . . .

There was a Convocation of students the first week, solemn and impressive. The faculty in their robes were on the stage. The auditorium was crowded with several thousand students. The organ rolled and thundered, and the university president delivered a ringing sermon entitled "Student Spine."

With something of the same reverence that I had once given to the man in the pulpit, I listened while he defined the perfect student as one who always did what he knew he ought to do. He sold me. I would be a doctor.

That night I sat down with a pencil and ruler and blocked out a schedule of my academic days that would have done credit to a Prussian drillmaster. Certain hours were devoted to the study of certain subjects, and if an hour appeared without something in it that I ought to be doing, I filled the space with "gymnasium" or "recreation." When I had finished budgeting my future academic time there was no niche or cranny of my life that made any allowance whatsoever for a sinner who liked to loaf, and my character was very similar to the old Fordson, or the old binder which never tied bundles according to plan.

In the rooming house where I had taken lodging there were seven freshmen, with their severed apron strings still dangling, one junior, and a senior Law student, all under one roof. Ten of us slept, after a fashion, in an attic arranged as a dormitory.

At night foreign objects appeared in beds, sheets were doubled back beneath blankets, jars of water were affixed to the light string which one pulled from the stairs below, and the sound of falling furniture, cascading water, and raucous hilarity seldom ceased before midnight. On the second floor, in our "study" rooms, cigarette butts scarred table tops, chairs were disabled in scuffling, and pictures of disrobed chorus girls were mounted directly on the wallpaper with gobs of paste.

The woman who owned, and who had expected to profit from, this dwelling, lived in a state of siege on the ground floor, where she cowered in impotent fear.

I did not stand aloofly to one side, doing only those things which I knew I ought to do. In fact it was my own thunderous execution of a double shuffle on my bedroom floor that brought the plaster down in the landlady's soup, and gave us all a bad afternoon in the Dean's office.

But the books were there, and my appetite was stronger than ever. The premedical sciences I studied provided my English themes with new weapons of Doubt, and nothing more. There was no appetite in me for the long life of drudgery that a doctor's career entailed, there was only an appetite for knocking down the tenpins of religious belief.

It was not at the moment fashionable to be studious. It was the era of Prohibition and John Held, Jr. The student called himself Joe College and he was strictly of the eat-drink-and-be-merry school of thought. He wore pebble-grain oxfords with hard leather heels, wool socks, no garters. He wore cream-colored suits, with wide trousers known as "Oxford bags." They drooped over one's shoes in front and swept the streets behind. With a thumb in each of his lower vest pockets the student walked erect with fluid knees and toes fanned wide in a sophisticated waddle known locally as the "Harvard strut." He was an epicure, a leisurely clubman who forswore earnestness and openly bragged that he "hadn't cracked a book."

I was first of all a conformist. My suits were cream colored and my pants swept the streets. I was one of the peas in the pod. If I was a little bowlegged, the pants hid it. On those occasions when I chanced to wear a hat, I intentionally curled its brim upward away from my eyes in a gesture characteristic of the countryside from which I hailed, because I was proud of being a Westerner, but most of the time I wore hair grease instead of a hat, and consequently I seldom had an opportunity to indulge this vanity. Indolence came readily to my disposition, particularly after a summer spent in haying and in shocking grain. In the matter of "cracking books" I succeeded in doing so inaudibly and with the expenditure of enough effort to avoid embarrassment in class and in examinations.

The showdown on medicine occurred at the end of my junior year. I met it by not entering my application, and informed my aunt and uncle by mail. I told them that I wasn't cut out to be a doctor, that I was going to be a writer instead. The following fall I elected journalism and writing courses, let the chips fall where they may.

But the fashion in authorship had changed in the interval between high-school graduation and college commencement, and it had become apparent that not all newspapermen became successful authors. All those I knew were sparrows, and their writing fell daily into trash receptacles. The fashion for college graduates, if one could trust F. Scott Fitzgerald and the rest, was to become a "customer's man" who utilized his college contacts to sell stocks and bonds on the booming stock market, or who went abroad to "find himself" in the culture of Europe. Most of the authors who were selling were over there, living gracefully.

I had no desire to become one among five million on New York City's streets, and I thought of Europe as a place where Renaissance kewpies were crowded cheek by jowl with mutilated Greek goddesses, where cathedrals were built of the bones of ancient pagan temples, and gravestones had been erected on the uneasy sites of buried gravestones. I had no desire to subject myself to these reminders of human defeat. A man who wants to leave footprints doesn't walk on trampled sands. I was going back to South Dakota.

But I couldn't tell the professor that I was going to be a Shakespeare or an Ezra Kind. As a writer I was no eagle, I was a foot pilgrim who had nothing to write about but Doubt. So I gave him some arithmetic instead, for the decision I was making seemed to call for some logical explanation.

"I've been looking at the sheep market," I said, "and I can see a ten thousand dollar gross on that place of mine if I work things right. It's my idea to build the ranch up into a paying proposition so I can sell it and write. By the time I get that done I'll have something to write about."

This union of hard headed commercialism with artistry-through-suffering resounded very pleasantly in my own ears, and I left the office feeling older and wiser and more bitter than I have ever succeeded in feeling since.

Chapter III

IT WAS neither a greenhorn nor an educated fool that bought a pickup truck to haul his bachelor's degree back to a South Dakota ranch; nor a leisurely clubman intent upon eating, drinking, and being merry before he died. I was an amateur geologist, chemist, physicist and author who thought his brain was equal to matching wits with the rigors of Dakota soil, and I was a Dakotan who knew from experience that Dakota was no toy. My vision was blurred by the pessimisms and the intellectual conceits to which adolescents are prone, but in a very practical and literal sense I knew who I was, where I was, and what I wanted to become.

In the three days it took me to reach my state line I drove through a land that was teeming with farms which were already paying businesses. I saw green fields tilled up to the very fence lines, neat red barns with tall silos beside them. Farm after farm after farm. There seemed to be a great many farms already in the world that were paying businesses. Some that I passed were for sale.

When I crossed the South Dakota line I saw no abrupt change in the prosperous appearance of the countryside. The fields of corn were just as green, the barns were just as red, the silos just as tall.

But slowly the trees dwindled in numbers, the red barns appeared now only in the valleys where streams flowed, and the silos disappeared altogether. There was also a noticeable change in the light. There was no longer a haze, the air was as clear as crystal, and under that light the sky line receded to greater and greater distances. The light beat down with a harsh frankness, denying the land the illusion of mystery which shade and shadow afford. There were no shadows, only the rolling prairie land, climbing and falling, mounting slowly under me, disappearing ahead against the sky.

The towns I passed suffered disparagement at the hands of the prairie and the light. They were stark, bleak, huddled, commonplace. They were thin towns whose means of support were not immediately visible to the eye. No silos fed them, only unpainted barns and gaunt ranch houses lonely against the sky.

As the miles accumulated on my speedometer, my mind began to weave under the impact of so many acres, of so much land. There were too many of these acres for any one acre to have either value or significance. There were too many hills for any one hill to claim admiration. The road climbed steadily the hill ahead, and although one hoped that the summit would achieve some climax, the climax always failed to occur.

As the hours gathered on my driving day, there came to me a feeling that I was in the presence of power, power which fought me and made demands upon me. The hills lifted and fell and crested again and tumbled away toward the sky line in a prodigal display of force. Though the eye saw the evidence of movement, nothing moved. This was movement translated into some superhuman phase of time. No human hour could measure its surging, the resonance of this lifting and falling was too deep a note for human ear, and no human mind could conceive of this tremendous surf being contained by any shore. I felt diminished, a small speck creeping across the face of something that was very large.

Toward evening I saw with gratitude the first black smudge that marked the Black Hills. Below that range of mountains was the town where I had graduated from high school. I beat toward it, as a mariner beats toward a landfall.

But this town was also strangely diminished, slowed and thinned. For my mind was still weaving with the motion of those prairie hills. I couldn't see the town as a passenger sees the deck of a vessel on which he rides, but as a gull sees a vessel far beneath him, dwarfed by the ocean on which it rides.

I passed through the town and went on. As I took the

road which climbed the hills toward the ranch, I was thoroughly weary of acres and of land. I thought, "How can my land have value when there is so much land?"

But when I topped the last hill and the familiar acres lay below me, the weaving of my mind was suddenly stilled. Nothing here had moved, nothing had changed. The long sweep of meadowland still led my eyes across my line fence to claim the distance-purpled Butte. The hills of my grazing land, now deep and mysterious in the shadow of evening, were a crested surf that beat at last upon a shore. For to the west there loomed the high, black mountains that to me had always meant home. The waves of prairie which had swept me westward all day had at last been contained. And Laddie, the collie dog, was waiting for me at the gate.

My overalls, worn and faded from many washings, were folded in my dresser drawer. My battered work hat hung on a nail in the woodshed. My old boots stood in a corner of the closet, toed in for a Dakotan's haste-driven amble, not outward for a clubman's leisurely strut. When I picked up the milk pail, it was as though it had never left my hands. When I pressed my head against the flank of the cow, and the sweet-smelling milk began to foam in the pail, Joe College was as far from my thoughts as the Dalai Lama of Tibet.

My welcome was not what I expected. The letters which Aunt Ida had written, and to which Uncle Harry had added his own comment, had been almost vehement in urging me to go on with medicine, or to get a job on a newspaper. I was braced for a continuation of that argument, and I was not prepared for the aura of gladness which surrounded my return. Seeing it, or rather feeling it, I began to understand what it had cost them to urge me not to return. They needed me.

The bad years which followed the collapse of the War Boom had eroded their savings and their vigor. As time passed there had been less and less money for hired help, and they had slowly withdrawn from the more ambitious intention with which they had arrived on the ranch. Neighbors were putting up the hay on shares and farming the fields on shares. The necessity of selling the entire calf crop year after year to meet indebtedness had reduced the beef herd to half its former size. But poultry was something they could handle themselves, without help, and they had done well with it. They wanted to continue with the poultry. What I wanted to do with the rest of it was up to me.

The disapproval of my return to ranching which I had expected from them, I found instead in the attitude of my neighbors and my friends in town. I had violated a principle of contemporary thinking — the local-boy-who-makes-good always does so in a big city, he doesn't come home to do it.

If there was any danger that my plan to run the ranch full tilt would peter out in indolence, here was a compulsion that would prevent it. For I had a bachelor of arts degree and whether I liked it or not, the quality of my ranching would be compared critically with that of men who had no education. There was no one watching me from the sky above the Butte, but my neighbors were, and I became acutely conscious of how my fields looked from the road.

It was my intention that the farming land should be black once more with full-sized bets on wheat and corn, and that sheep would replace the cattle on the grazing land on the south half of the ranch. Mid-June was too late for a farming venture, but the alfalfa and wild hay promised a long and heavy haying season, and the first step I planned to take was to get rid of horses from the hayfield.

When we had moved on the ranch eight years before there were twenty-five head of horses on the place. There had been one good team, three poor teams, and a string of tall rangy geldings which had never been broken to harness. There was a one-eyed mare whose eye had been torn out on a harness hook when she was being broken years before. She was dangerous, and when she had the opportunity, struck with both front feet. One of the teams, though it was gentle and old enough to vote, ran away with whatever they were hitched to, whenever they were hitched to it. Tiring of the wreckage, Uncle Harry had sold them the first summer, but before the buyer got them off the place, they ran away with his wagon and wiped out a row of corral posts like ninepins. The geldings were too old to break by the time we came to the ranch, and they spent a carefree life, rampaging around like hoodlums, alert for a gate that was open, or rubbing their buttocks on the carriage shed until it eventually collapsed. Uncle Harry had been slow in getting rid of them because my dad had done a good job on their breeding and he was reluctant to take the loss that others' carelessness had cost.

"Your dad was a good hand with horses," he told me one day. "One of the best I ever saw, but he couldn't get the renter's boys to do it his way. He used to come down here to do the breaking himself when he could. That one-eyed mare bunged him up pretty bad one day."

I remembered something of that incident. It had impressed my seven-year-old mind more perhaps because it was the first time I had even suspected that my dad could be hurt by anything. I was used to seeing him dressed and acting in a certain way, and it was a shock to see him with a black eye and limping up the steps.

Usually his clothing was spotless and undisturbed. His shoes were always shined, his brown mustache was trimmed, and when he met a woman on the street he took off his derby hat with a flourish that was half a bow. He didn't get mad very often, but when Mother laughed at his black eye he was mad and said, "It ain't funny."

And it wasn't. His face was bruised in other places too, and he hadn't been able to shave. His ribs were taped and he had to limp.

My mother saw that it wasn't funny. "What on earth happened to you?" she asked.

"Those damned kids bunged up a mare," he said. "They tried to handle her when I wasn't there. I tried to get a look at her and when I got almost up to her, she knocked me down and walked on me. It wasn't her fault — you'd be mad too if somebody had knocked your eye out on a nail."

A little while after that Dad went to Mayos' and when he came back I was even more disturbed by the news that we might have to move away.

Ordinarily my mother and father and I slept in a large bedroom. In one corner was the double bed which Dad and Mother occupied. In the other corner, parallel to it, was my bed. There was a big coal heater in the center of the room, beside it a pail of coal and another of kindling. Throughout the winter we always slept with the window open. The first thing in the morning Dad would hop out of bed, slam the window down, shove kindling into the stove, thrust a crumpled newspaper into the lower draft, touch a match to it, and leap back into bed. At this point I usually left my own bed and joined them.

It was a pleasant thing to lie there listening to the fire roar in the chimney, while outside Mr. Williams, the neighbor next door, shoveled off his walk with an iron scoop. The sound of that scoop ringing on the cement was one that echoed long in my ears.

On the morning after Dad came back from the Mayo Clinic at Rochester, the fire roared in the chimney as usual, but Dad hadn't built it. Mother built it, and got back into bed. Dad was sick.

"George," she said to him, "what do they think caused it? Was it that time the mare ran over you down at the ranch?"

"No," Dad said, "my machinery is wearing out a little is all."

"Well," Mother said, "whatever caused it, if they told you to move to a lower altitude, that's what we'll have to do."

"To hell with it," Dad said. "I've got too many irons in the fire. I might as well die here as starve to death in some country where I don't know the ropes."

The word death did not occur to me, even then. The words I feared were "going away."

But we weren't going away, so it was all right.

Summer had exchanged Mr. Williams' snow shovel for a broom, and flower-picking time had obscured the memory of snow-covered streets when sickness came again to our house. This time Mother was sick.

For three days I stayed at Aunt Ida's house in the Fourth Ward. It was near the hospital. My mother was in the hospital and the rest of us stayed at Aunt Ida's so it wouldn't be far from Mother's room in case anything went wrong.

At the end of three days I was homesick and weary of the situation. Without feeling any real sense of peril, I was tired of being where I was and wanted to go home. I told my aunt as much.

"What a way for you to talk!" she said. "Your mother is

an awfully sick woman. You eat your oatmeal now, and when I go up to the hospital I'll see if you may come up to visit her today."

"I don't want to visit her," I said. "I want to go home."

"But you can't go home!" Aunt Ida stated. "The house is locked and there's nobody there."

"Then I'm going to Crystal Cave and get some of those crystals. The rest of the kids got some the other day."

Aunt Ida exploded. "If you budge out of this yard," she said emphatically, "I'll see that you're soundly thrashed!"

I studied the carpet while she put on her hat and veil to go up to the hospital. With a perfunctory kiss for me, and a worried frown for my mother, she hastened out the door.

When she was out of sight I opened the gate and went home.

The house was locked and all the blinds were down. I tried the back door and couldn't get in. I sat down on the front step with my chin in my hands. Then I saw Lyle across the street.

"Hello, Reefus," he said. "How's your mother?"

"She's pretty good," I said. "Let's go to Crystal Cave today and get some of those crystals."

"You have to have a lunch to go to Crystal Cave," he objected. "It's a long ways."

"We can take some potatoes and bake 'em in a fire," I suggested.

The suggestion took root. Not long afterward Lyle and

I and three other boys, our pockets bulging with potatoes, started down through the First Ward on our way to Crystal Cave. We passed the Round House where Mr. Williams worked and took the railroad tracks when the road left the creek. We went on down past the slag pile to the city dump. There was a pond below the dump in which there were pollywogs. We took off our shoes and stockings and waded there in the warm water, catching pollywogs. We were still wading when the Round House whistle blew for noon.

My heart sank. I was not supposed to be wading, I was supposed to be in Aunt Ida's yard.

"Come on, kids!" I said. "Let's hurry up and get to Crystal Cave and get back. I'm going to catch it!"

They were in no hurry. They built a fire to bake the potatoes. We were squatting around it when Mr. Williams came down the tracks. He stopped and looked us all over before his eye finally found me.

"Young man," he said angrily, "do you know that your mother is dead and that your father is half crazy trying to find you?"

"My mother ain't either dead," I said. "She's up at the hospital."

I thought he was just trying to scare me. But, although I didn't believe a word of it, I started to cry. Crying, I followed him up the tracks.

My father and his partner, Jerome, were sitting in a Transfer rig where the road ended near the Round House.

Dad came down the tracks to meet me, and took my hand. His eyes were swollen and red, and his jaw muscles stood out the way they did sometimes when he was going to lick me. But he didn't lick me.

He stopped his tears with a handkerchief, blew his nose and put the handkerchief back in his pocket. Then he lifted me up into the rig. We drove at a trot up through the First Ward.

"Jerome," Dad said, "I'm going to have to sell out. Do you reckon you can raise the wind to buy my half?"

"I reckon I can buy you out," Jerome answered, "but I don't think I could swing it to buy the ranch."

"The ranch isn't for sale," Dad said. "Harry and I have a good man on it, and it'll be worth a lot of money some day. I'm going to keep the ranch for George."

"It don't seem right to talk about those things," Jerome said, "so soon after. . . ."

"I can't help it," Dad said. "I've got to step around now. I was the one that was supposed to die. Now I've got to stay alive. George and I are going to Florida just as soon as — this is over."

So my third-grade studies in geography were interrupted by geography itself. When the freight car had been loaded with our furniture, and Little Dick was led into the stall they had fixed for him in the middle of the car, we packed our suitcases at Aunt Ida's, and Jerome took us to the six o'clock train. Twenty-five hundred miles later we were in Florida.

Our first night in Florida was spent in a hotel room. There was a mosquito netting over the bed, and more netting at the windows. Rain fell outside in an unending downpour, but the air in the room was hot and close.

In the middle of the night I wakened to find that Dad was choking for air. He told me to get a doctor, quick. I knew as well as he did what we were up against because he had told me in detail, as matter-of-factly as though we were talking about a horse on the ranch. So I was afraid, more so because he was afraid.

The hall outside was dark and the hotel was still. But there was a light on in the room next to ours. I banged on the door and a man without any shirt on answered my knock. I told him that my dad was dying and needed a doctor. He got a doctor.

The doctor gave Dad some medicine and stayed until daylight. In a couple of days we were able to leave the hotel and move into a house. Dad said that the lower altitude was beginning to take hold.

When summer came in Florida, it was not with the cool rains and fresh breezes which we had known in Deadwood, but with a heavy, oppressive heat from which there was no respite even at night.

"To hell with this country," Dad said. "We'll move in with my brother up in Kentucky and maybe buy a place there. How'd you like to go into the horse business in the Blue Grass, son?"

"I'd rather go home," I said.

Dad made no reply.

In Kentucky we drove about a great deal with my Uncle Bill, riding in a runabout behind Little Dick.

Once, when we were driving away from a place which Dad had looked over from one end to the other, he said, discontentedly, "This country is smaller than I remember it. Hell, there ain't room to turn a six-horse team."

"There's a bigger place up near Cynthiana," Uncle Bill replied. "We can take a train up there and hire a rig."

"Ain't that near where we used to live?" Dad asked.

Uncle Bill nodded. "And right on the edge of the Blue Grass," he said.

There was no one home, and as we prowled the place, Dad began to sound a little more like himself.

"I could put in some brood mares and raise registered Percherons," he mused, "and if I could get Harry to handle it from the other end, we might run it up into a fair business. That Dakota country up there needs big work stock, but nobody seems to have time to do it. . . ."

We looked some more, then Dad said, "This is going to cost some money. I want to send some wires before I go out on a limb with a down payment."

A couple of hours later we stopped at a railroad station, and while Uncle Bill stayed with the horses, Dad and I went in.

There was a man in a green eyeshade behind the grilled window.

"How about letting me send it myself?" Dad asked.

The man looked at him for a moment. "Sure," he said, "come on in and make yourself at home."

Dad went in and stood beside the table of noisy instruments.

"Which way had I better go for Deadwood, South Dakota?" he asked.

"Chicago and Omaha," said the operator.

"Omaha!" Dad said with a broad smile. "By golly, it's a small world!"

The instruments clattered and Dad turned to me.

"Hear that, son? That's Deadwood. Deadwood, South Dakota!"

The instrument clattered in his own fingers, then he waited for a reply. Something was going on that was over my head. Dad laughed and the operator laughed and said, "Deadwood is quite a josher!"

When we left, Dad was feeling better than he had felt for a long time, the sharp look had come back to the corners of his eyes, and he told Uncle Bill that before long Kentucky was going to see some nice big draft stock for a change.

But that night Dad couldn't breathe again. We had a doctor, and medicine, and burned some stuff in a saucer under Dad's nose. We bought no land in the Blue Grass, but went back to Florida instead.

That winter, for the first time in two years, I saw snow. A playmate came by our house about half an hour before school one morning with the news that snow was to be seen down at the railroad tracks where a train had set out some boxcars during the night.

My haste was almost too much for my leisurely playmate, and after all, he had already seen the snow. But he kept up with me, and we pushed in through a crowd of other boys to look at the wonder.

I was disappointed. There wasn't enough of it to do anything with, just a little heap on the couplings between the cars. But it was snow, and Dad, I knew, was homesick for some snow. So I filled a tomato can with some and hastened home with it.

Dad stuck his finger down in the can and dug the snow with his fingernail. Then he emptied the can and wrung a snowball out of it. He hurled the snowball at an orange tree.

Not long after that Dad told me we were going to move again.

"Are we going back to Deadwood?" I asked.

"Not so fast," he cautioned me. "There's a doctor in Frisco that says he can cure hardening of the arteries. We'll go out to California and get cured, then we'll go home."

We moved into a flat in Berkeley, California, within easy commuting distance of the doctor's office in San Francisco. There were mountains around the town, but they were not like my native mountains, and they were too far away. Those that I could reach on foot bore "no trespassing" signs. It wasn't mountains that I wanted, but special mountains, White Rocks for example.

On Saturdays I went to Frisco with Dad and waited for him in the doctor's office while he sat under the machine that "set up the sympathetic vibration of electrons" and cured hardening of the arteries. Afterward we went to a show, sometimes William S. Hart, or Dustin Farnum. *The Birth of a Nation* we saw twice.

When school was out we moved to Frisco, taking a room in an apartment house where the doctor's nurse lived. We ate our meals with her, and slept in our own bedroom. Dad was getting better all the time.

Every morning Dad gave me fifty cents to go to the World's Fair and his nurse packed a lunch for me. It cost a nickel to ride to the grounds, and a quarter to get in. That left fifteen cents for the Midway and a nickel to get home. Sometimes the guard winked and shoved me under the turnstile for nothing. On those days I saw the Grand Canyon or some other show that cost a quarter.

When my money was gone I went to work on the souvenirs. I prowled every corner of the fair grounds in search of postcards, dangling trinkets, and printed give-aways of every form and description. Before long the floor of our clothes closet completely disappeared.

But in time the hunt slackened, and one day I seated myself before a typewriter in the Underwood exhibit. Slipping a sheet of paper into the machine I wrote: "Dear Uncle Harry and Aunt Ida: I sure would like to see that snow you wrote to Dad about. Maybe Dad and I will get home so I can shovel it off before it melts. I won't charge you anything. Your nephew George."

A little while later we moved to a town about a hundred miles south of San Francisco. Two nurses ran a rest home there. Dad needed a rest home because he was tired a lot of the time, and the nurses could arrange things so he didn't have to do much. On the other hand, it wouldn't cost a fortune, like living in the hospital all the time.

The town was quite a bit like Deadwood. The hills rose steeply on either side of a brick-paved Main Street and the hoofs of the delivery horses sounded just exactly the same as they had at home. But there wasn't any snow to shovel off the walks.

Then one day there was snow — not in town, but within sight of the town. On a mountainside, in plain view of the rest home, I could see a field that was white with it.

Immediately a bunch of us started out with the idea that we would build a snow fort. But when we arrived the sun had reduced the snow to slush, and there wasn't enough left to do anything with. But under the trees which bordered the field I found enough to carry some home to Dad.

Arrived home, I made a beeline for his room, but the nurse stopped me at the door.

"You'd better not go in now," she said, "your father has just had a hypodermic."

The snowball melted on the porch. Night fell. I learned

that I was not to sleep in the room with Dad, but in the parlor on a couch.

Very late in the night I was awakened by the doctor passing through into Dad's room. He came out and went away. Then the nurse came out. She grabbed me around the neck and began to cry.

So Dad and I went home.

The morning after the funeral I ate my oatmeal and drank my cocoa. Uncle Harry showed me where the snow shovel was kept, and went off to work. I took the snow shovel and dragged it behind me out to the walk. But just as I was getting to work an old man came down the street and stopped to talk.

"What have you got there?" he asked, standing right in my way.

"A snow shovel," I replied. "I'm going to shovel off the walk."

"Do you know what the Injuns says about shoveling off walks?"

"No," I said politely, "I never heard."

"Injun says 'Ugh! Paleface heap big fool. Injun let sun shovel off the walk!' "

"Humph!" I said. "It ain't any fun when the sun melts it."

He went on down the street and I set the shovel to scraping the walk.

The shovel scraped loudly on the cement, and it didn't sound the way it had sounded when Mr. Williams used to shovel off the walk. It was also hard work. I threw the shovel down and looked up at the rimrock where the pines stared down upon the town. The sky was overcast and a restless wind was roaring through the trees on the mountain tops. I had lost my gun, there was nothing to eat, and I was alone.

Some years later I saw the brief record of that journey in a sheaf of telegrams in a pigeonhole of my uncle's desk. They were clipped together in chronological sequence. The first read, "Kissimmee Fla. Sept. 20, 1912. Car arrived safely. Tell Charley to add 5 to Jacksonville rate. George." The next one read, "Cynthiana Kentucky, July 12, 1913. See opportunity here breeding work stock for sale there. Can't swing deal alone. Can you raise five thousand and handle marketing there. George." The third was from Berkeley, California, "Doctor bills are fierce. Can you sell team of blacks for five hundred. George." The fourth and last one read, "G. M. Reeves passed away 2 A.M. Come. C. H. Krause."

Some of this may have been in Uncle Harry's mind when he kept that string of well-bred, worthless outlaws and permitted them to board on good grass for nothing, but it wasn't in my mind at all when I sold them.

The thing that was fresh in my memory was the job of making hay with work horses. First one had to catch a saddle horse from the small pasture, saddle it, ride the big pasture until the herd was found, and drive them all in through the corral gate despite their canny efforts to avoid a day of labor. The work team had to be caught from the bunch, one at a time with a halter. Tied in their stalls, they were fed oats and curried. The next step was to clean the dried horsehair from the inside of the collar and buckle it on the horse's neck with the pole strap dangling between the horse's fore legs. Then one took the harness off the hook, spread it on the horse's back, fitted the hames to the collar, buckled them, reached for the pole strap with one hand and the near hold-back strap with the other. When the hold-back straps were snapped to the pole strap, one buckled the bellyband, took off the halter, and put on the bridle. When the team was harnessed one led the first horse out, went back for the second, took down the lines, snapped the lines to the bridles, drove the team over the tongue, fitted the neckyoke first to the pole straps, then to the breast straps which dangled from the hames, fitted the neckyoke to the tongue, and at last hooked up the tugs.

An ignition key was the answer, and the sons of the one-eyed mare went down the road to a buyer who had lions to feed in the St. Louis Zoo.

❦❦❦❦❦❦❦❦❦❦❦

Chapter IV

ANGEL WITH A SWORD

❦❦❦❦❦❦❦❦❦❦❦

THERE was a new tractor on the market which I coveted. Called the "Farmall," it had been designed for all-year use. As nimble in haying and cultivating as it was powerful on plow and disc, I was convinced that it was a tool that would dominate the tide of plenty that so many times had slipped through our fingers.

When I first saw it in the dealer's yard, there was a seven-foot mower mounted on its drawbar. I bought the outfit, mower and all.

It was a far cry from this seven-foot swath to that of the old four-foot machines which my father and grandfather had used; and it was a sharp improvement over the complex system of tongues and clevises by which we had hitched two mowers to the old Fordson the previous summer. At five miles an hour the new tractor marched down the field, tumbling a deep swath behind it. Where a team wallowed around the corners, the Farmall snapped sharply and was off again on the new swath. Furthermore, its vigorous engine did not begrudge pulling a rake at the same time.

Mounted on this tractor with a rake behind it, I could cut and rake as much hay in a day as the renter's four boys had done with four teams.

But though I could mow and rake hay at this phenomenal speed, stacking was slow. I still had horses on the sweep and on the stacker rope. And I still retained some of the work habits that I had acquired in four years at college — unconsciously I put off any unpleasant task as long as possible, just as I had put off studying until the day before the examination.

Unfortunately, hay couldn't be "crammed" into the stack, and there were no fixed dates in haying season. There were only still days and windy days, dry days and wet days, and sometimes a day might change its mind at noon. The result was that some of my hay moulded in the windrow, some in the shock, and some of it I cut after frost.

My attitude toward my uncle, through all this, was a curious mixture of affection and scorn. Mistakes that he had made in his eight years of tenure were everywhere apparent, and as an amateur scientist, I could not cheerfully tolerate mistakes in any form. I overruled him in matters of policy with the firm indulgence that a wise parent bestows upon a subnormal child.

It would have been hard, even for a celestial observer, to have seen in this graying man the demigod, who, when I was living with my parents on Williams Street, had dispensed nickels from a tremendous fortune in small change which he carried in his pants pocket; or to have seen in my financially subdued partner the "new father," who, on that bleak day in January of 1916, when the snow shovel had failed my homecoming, paid me a quarter to finish shoveling off the walk. That quarter had marked the beginning of a complex affection through which worship and disapproval had ebbed and flowed for ten years. If 1926 was a bad year for demigods, 1916 was a good one for a new father, and some of it was still alive when I came home from school.

On the first day of that twenty-five-cent relationship, Uncle Harry came home at three, and after paying me my quarter he said, "How would you like to go up on the hill for a little target practice?"

"Target practice?" I said. "You mean with a *gun?*"

He went to the closet, and my eyes opened wide when he came out with a .22 rifle.

"Can I shoot it?" I asked.

"You bet you can," he said, "and it'll be your gun after you're old enough to use it."

We lived on Lincoln Avenue and the place to go to shoot a gun was up on the hill. We soon left the sidewalks behind and plodded through unmarked snow under the pines.

"This is sure better than California," I said. "Heck, in California whenever I tried to go out to find some place to pick flowers or something, all I could see was signs saying keep off."

71

"No 'keep off' signs on this timber," Uncle Harry said. "This is Forest Reserve, and it belongs to everybody. You've got Teddy Roosevelt to thank for that. He made it a National Forest about the time you were born."

"I sure do thank him," I said. "When can we shoot the gun?"

An hour or so later, as we came back down the hill toward home, I said, "Uncle Harry, do you know how to get to Crystal Cave?"

"I was down there once on a saddle horse when I was a boy," he replied. "I'll take you down there one of these days."

We went down past the Round House and the slag pile and the city dump. Uncle Harry was on afternoon shift now, and we had to get back before three o'clock.

We followed the railroad track for a long way, and his eyes scanned the base of the rimrock for the dark opening of the cave. Several times we thought we saw it, but when we had climbed the steep side of the gulch, we found only small bugholes in the limestone cliffs, not Crystal Cave.

At last he looked at his watch and said, "We've got to be getting back."

The following Saturday I set out with five companions, several of whom had been to Crystal Cave. We carried lunches, matches, and a belt axe to cut pitch torches for the trip into the cave. We walked several miles beyond the point where Uncle Harry had begun to search, and at last we spied the trail that led upward to the cave entrance.

The entrance was an arched room, soot-blackened by many campfires, and by the initials of previous visitors who had smoked them there by holding candles near the stone. We cut torches and went into the echoing depths of the cave. The walls were covered with crystals, and the floor was thick with them, in truckloads. Gloating briefly over this wealth, and filling our pockets with it, we returned to the entrance to roast our wieners over a fire.

Seated by the fire munching a wiener sandwich, I felt sorry for Uncle Harry because he had to work, and for not knowing where Crystal Cave was.

That night I told him where it was, and demonstrated with pencil and paper where he had made his mistake. Then I added, in a kindlier tone, "It's probably been a long time since you were down there, and things like that are hard to remember."

It was harder to be tolerant of Uncle Harry's mistakes in driving the new Ford. I went along when the dealer delivered it, listening with sharp ears from the back seat as the dealer explained the array of foot pedals by which it shifted into reverse, or braked, or lurched into high gear.

When Uncle Harry took over the wheel, he pushed the wrong pedal and the engine died.

"Oh — oh," said the dealer, "you killed it!"

When the fine point of forward motion had apparently

been mastered, the dealer took his departure. When we were alone, Uncle Harry again pushed the wrong pedal.

"Oh — oh," I said, "you killed it!"

"I know it," said Uncle Harry, a little grimly perhaps.

When the motor was roaring again, and the car had successfully made its flying leap into high gear, we started for Lead City where the company offices were, and where Uncle Harry was going to collect his bimonthly pay.

There, headed the wrong way on a street that ended in the Open Cut, we had to turn around or stay there. Uncle Harry experimented with the reverse pedal, and vigorously cramped the wheels. But after half an hour, we were still heading the wrong way.

Our rescue was abrupt, unexpected, but complete. A gang of Slavonian miners, on their way to work, had solemnly observed our difficulties from the sidewalk. Suddenly they left the walk, surrounded the car, lifted it, turned it around, and dropped it with a bounce back on its wheels.

"Better you get a horse," the leader growled as they took their departure.

"You didn't turn the wheels the right way," I said, truthfully, when our rescuers had gone.

"Goddamit, shut up!" was his answer, and for two years — thanks to his bullheaded determination that I was too young to learn to drive — I never sat beneath the steering wheel while the car was in motion.

But if he got to the steering wheel first, it was I who got

to the ranching first. Uncle Harry was a mining man and he had never had much time to go to the ranch. Before we got the car the only way to get there was to go down to Rapid City on the train, hire a rig and drive out. It was a three-day trip that way and Uncle Harry could seldom leave his job with the company for that long. When my dad was alive, he had been the one to go to the ranch, and since then the renters had been running things pretty much to suit themselves.

On his first "Long Change" at the plant, Uncle Harry and Aunt Ida and I drove down in the new Ford. While the renter stood with his foot on the fender telling Uncle Harry about the new machinery he needed to run the place right, I vanished with the renter's youngest boy to have a ride on the pony.

When the time came to leave I was reluctant to depart from a place on which there was a pony, with the result that the car departed without me. Thus it came about that I was on the spot to help set up the new machinery when it arrived, and I knew how it worked long before Uncle Harry had laid eyes upon it.

The mower and rake and binder were complete when they arrived, but the sweep and stacker had to be assembled from a pile of painted lumber which the implement men had simply dumped on the ground.

Slowly the sweep began to take shape. Long wooden teeth reached out in front to run under the shocked hay, and piled it up against a framework of boards. Twelve feet wide, there was a place for one horse on each edge behind the teeth. The driver rode a seat on the back end, with levers before him to raise or lower the teeth. Once the load was shoved onto the teeth, he raised it from the ground with the levers and small wheels carried the weight on the long trip in to the stacker. The wheels in back turned at will in any direction, making it possible to stop one horse, whip the other, and turn the whole affair in a small circle.

The stacker had similar teeth upon which the load was deposited by dropping the sweep teeth. Then a system of pulleys, powered by a stacker team, catapulted the load of hay onto the stack, where a man kept it in order with a hay fork.

It had been the general idea that I could drive this stacker team, so that two of the boys could go on mowing while the other two stacked. Unfortunately, the first time I drove the stacker team, I drove them ten feet too far, the rope broke, and suddenly the new stacker was a pile of splinters.

The renter's reaction was something less than kindly and affectionate. While curses filled the air, and two of the boys prowled through the wreckage to discover what timbers had to be replaced, the renter told me to get on that goddam pony and keep to hell out of the goddam way.

Suddenly I was as homesick for the affection of my aunt and uncle as ever I had been for the sound of a snow shovel scraping on a cement walk, and not long afterward I went to Deadwood.

ANGEL WITH A SWORD

So 1916 earned me two well-deserved cursings, but it had also earned me a blessing or two, and on Christmas morning I found the .22 rifle under the tree. It may be that I owed these things to the death of my father, and my birth to the death of Ezra Kind, but the obligation of which I was conscious was to a man in a corduroy suit who had paid me a quarter for shoveling off his walk, and if in 1926 I thought he was a fool, my affection for him was not lessened thereby.

But a practicing scientific thinker does not permit sentiment to interfere with his perception of truth, nor does he accept advice from one who has been so frequently mistaken. Uncle Harry thought I ought to go around and talk to a few sheepmen before I bought any sheep, but I had no more confidence in the advice of neighboring sheepmen than I had in his. Instead I bought a book.

That fall I bought my sheep. Having read and digested *three* books on sheep, I felt that I was ready to buy a band.

When a man showed me a band of sheep he had for sale, I didn't ask him about his sheep, instead I proved to him that I had read the text.

It may have been the seller's intention to warn me that the ewes he had for sale were culls from a big Montana herd, that they were being sold solely because they were "drys" which for many reasons best known to themselves hadn't raised lambs. It may have been his intention to tell me that while on the way to the railhead they had become tangled with a big buck herd and that they were probably

bred for January lambs. But if he had earnestly desired to
come clean, he had no opportunity to do so, for I was on the
air, and I was doing the talking.

In January the sheep began to do the talking.

One cold, subzero morning I stepped into the barn and
heard a high, thin wail. In a hospital that sound would
have brought a nurse on the run. In the sheep barn in January I only stared.

Rounding a corner I saw a ewe bending over a newborn
lamb, talking to it, lapping it with her tongue. I looked
down upon a small creature whose eyes still swam with the
dark distances of the womb. Weaving its head back and
forth, it wailed again, and thrust itself to its feet. *A ewe
that belonged to me had reproduced itself!*

It didn't enter my head what this arrival might portend,
or that more practical and immediate thinking was called
for.

Three more lambs came that day. I pored over my sheep
books, and, obeying instructions, penned the ewes in individual pens with their lambs. But the mothers had no milk
— their bags were hard as rocks. Some didn't even have
teats, having lost them in the shearing barn, or in some previous lambing mishap.

I built a small bum pen and put the orphans on a diet of
cow's milk.

The next morning when I entered the barn I discovered
that I had been unwise to go to bed at all. The shed was
literally alive with newborn lambs. They lay everywhere,

in various stages of discontent and repair. Here and there
a mother was cleaning her lamb, but most of the ewes had
walked away and were unconcernedly chewing their cuds.
The telltale signs of birth could be seen scattered through
the band, but the offspring lay untended in small pools of
birth fluid. Which of the lambs belonged to which of the
ewes, there was no way of knowing.

There followed one of the most nerve-racking tasks I
have ever attempted. I tried to mate sixteen unclaimed
lambs with sixteen indifferent, noncommittal mothers. The
mathematical possibilities in this situation were staggering,
but I believe that I tried most of them. I walked endlessly
up and down the pens, trying lambs on ewes, then watching
for the faintest flicker of recognition. After two hours I had
arrived nowhere. Some of the lambs had meanwhile departed this life, the rest were about to do so. I ended by
hastening the survivors into the bum pen, where I had a
fire in the stove. As I deposited the newcomers I observed
that my old customers were all dead. But I had no time to
mourn, for more lambs were arriving in the shed.

From that time on I was the center of a maelstrom of
arriving life. It beat upon me with the weight of an ava-
lanche. It nearly flattened me completely. It worked me
twenty hours a day and worried me the other four. I worked
in an atmosphere of the bleakest kind of failure — a harvest
of dead and dying lambs. I couldn't turn to hired men for
help, for I was too ignorant myself to give them orders.
Meanwhile, if I tried to excuse myself on the grounds of

ignorance and by recalling that it was only money I was losing, the thin wails and pathetic forms of doomed lambs called me a liar. My business was too close to the entrances and exits of life to permit me the luxury of indifference.

Slowly I gained a little experience. Pulling the band in from pasture, I held them in the corrals on hay. I built more lambing pens and learned to keep the bums alive on cow's milk. I set the hired man to pouring hay into the ewes in an effort to improve the milk flow. It improved slowly, in those ewes capable of giving milk at all, the others simply fattened on the feed and admired me with friendly eyes. I added grain to the ration and inevitably fed too much. As a result many of the ewes began to slip their wool, leaving long strings of it on posts and on the wire fencing. At the end of six weeks I had lost ten pounds, and my band of sheep, disrobed, disgruntled, all but dismantled, was the laughingstock of my non-diplomaed neighborhood.

Then Dakota hit me again.

Theoretically April is not a winter month. April showers bring May flowers, not four feet of snow.

But the showers this April turned to snow. For six days the snow fell without stopping. There was no wind, no sun, no movement but the gentle piling of snow. At the end of the six days fifty-seven inches of snow buried my acres under a mantle that was completely and utterly paralyzing. Not even a saddle horse could wallow through it.

By the third day of the snowfall I was out of hay. There was none in the barn, and there was none in the fields —

my unplanned January lambing had used all my hay. There was only a straw stack, and that was two miles away.

I put the sheep on a straight grain diet. The hired man and I would walk through the shed with bushel baskets and pour out the grain in a long stream on the slimy floor. The ewes fought for it, trampling a third of it to unpalatability, then followed me clamoring.

On the sixth day the sun came out and the glare was unbearable. There was no break in the whiteness anywhere. Slowly the snow sank, a few inches a day, while the sheep stood trapped in the barn in humid heat and starved. On the ninth day the snow had sunk two feet and I reached the straw stack with a light wagon. I came home with a pitiful dab of straw and threw it on the barn floor. The sheep ate it, slime and all, and then followed me begging for more. They plucked at my buttons, they pulled cigarette papers out of my fingers, there was no end to their accusation.

When on the fifteenth day the gaunt survivors tottered out to grass, I hauled away three heaping wagonloads of carrion.

This was no tolerant, well-intentioned spanking, it was a heedless brutal clubbing, and it hurt. It had wiped out my margin of safety at one blow. I could look back with nostalgia upon the careless, half-contemptuous leisure of the college campus, and ahead to a future that differed in no essential particular from shoveling coal into engines or husking corn.

⊛〜⊙〜⊙〜⊙〜⊙〜⊙〜⊙〜⊙〜⊙〜⊙〜⊙〜⊙〜⊙

Chapter V

JUG BENEATH THE BOUGH

⊛〜⊙〜⊙〜⊙〜⊙〜⊙〜⊙〜⊙〜⊙〜⊙〜⊙〜⊙〜⊙

THERE WERE NO bruises on my pelt and I had no broken bones but I was dog-tired and my college diploma had taken a spanking in public. As a college graduate, my pride ached badly in several places. On sleepless nights I writhed a little at the thought that I might even now be continuing comfortably with the study of medicine, and then, when I rolled over to try for sleep on the other side, it pained me just as badly to think that I was not using my education on a city daily. Anywhere but here. As a rancher I had made every mistake in the book, and at two A.M. my failures looked less like cause and effect, and more like crime and punishment.

The world shaking philosophy which I had discovered in my sophomore themes didn't seem to yield much comfort in this its first real situation. In writing it had seemed infinitely fair and just that the Law of the Survival of the Fittest should be the agency of world improvement, but now that I seemed to be scheduled for nonsurvival, some part of my mind insisted that it was a hell of a way to run a world. Those long-winded pronouncements, in which I had proved to my own satisfaction that there is no such thing as choice or free will, didn't seem to save me from conse-

quences, even though it might be true that I was the creature of my heredity and my environment. In the belea-
guered sheepshed, while fifty-four inches of environment
surrounded the empty hayloft of my heredity, it was easy
enough to see some of the days on which I might have
chosen to fill the hayloft, and the sensations I felt were
those of responsibility. No matter what logic might be able
to prove in the matter of simple cause and effect, my pride
knew that it was being punished.

The whole matter of making some adjustment to this
punishment was on a bigger scale than any similar situation I had met before. The thing was done, the sheep were
dead, the lamb crop was poor, and I had lost a lot of money.
Another lamb crop was a year away, and a whole year is a
long time to promise to "behave."

My mother had spanked me into such a promise once,
and she had been downright vigorous about it. Memory of
the crime escapes me, but it must have been felonious to
have earned a hairbrush "on the raw." As a wide area of my
posterior grew unbelievably hot, I felt that I *had* to escape, but all I could do was wriggle in the hope that I could
deflect her aim to some relatively cooler spot. However,
she had a firm grip on my middle and her aim continued
good. When I recognized that I couldn't escape and that
hot was becoming infinitely hotter, I still persisted in believing that there was some way out. I turned my attention
to yelling, and that was it, when I yelled loud enough she
stopped.

Later, when the theory of hell-fire alarmed me briefly, I made a similar adjustment. It was my first day in Sunday school,I had been washed and starched within an inch of immobility. It was a hot July day and hell was not hard to imagine.

The Sunday school teacher had on a purple silk dress that whistled when she moved, and its collar came way up on her neck under her ears where it stopped just in time to let her chin stick out. She wore earrings too. The earrings and collar looked as though they hurt.

I tried to move to ease an itch, but my pants stuck to the varnish. I worked them loose and eased the place that itched as the woman began to talk.

She said that the Lord Jesus had given us all souls. She said that our souls were white and unwrinkled. Our Maker, and the Lord Jesus, wanted us to keep them white and unwrinkled. But if we were mean to the cat, or lied to our parents, wrinkles came on our souls. Then if we died in the night and were dragged before our Maker in Judgment, we would be thrown into hell to fry forever.

There was more of this, with the result that the first snapshot I took of God was not a flattering portrait. I saw an immense and terrible figure who never smiled or joked, who was only intent that I praise and obey Him. He never said, "Oh, that's all right, it really doesn't matter." To Him everything mattered, there was no relenting, no room in which a free spirit could move. There was in me at the very outset a distinct feeling of being pushed around. It did not seem to me right that anyone should be spanked forever. It did not seem possible that anybody could stay mad long enough to do it. I accepted it as true, but I didn't like it, and I didn't see why I should praise God if He was that hard to get along with.

Behind the Ten Commandments, and I came to them very early, I saw that same hard, unrelenting face. Under the circumstances I decided to run a bill. My death was probably remote and there would be plenty of time to square things before I was dragged before my Maker in Judgment.

"Dad," I said one night, out of a clear sky, "how do you commit adultery?"

He grunted in surprise.

"Adultery?" he said. "Oh, that's when you run off with another man's wife."

I was disappointed. It had sounded like something that might be fun. But if it wasn't fun, why have a Commandment? No telling why, some idea of God's perhaps.

But if the Ten Commandments failed to dominate my evil intentions, and the Sunday school teacher's parable yielded small comfort to our own cat, my formal education soon fell into the hands of experts who had no illusions about my dishonesty or my capacity to sin. These professionals refused to extend any credit, if I sinned the blow fell, now.

The schoolroom had a set of commandments tailored to fit, and backed by a cash-on-the-barrelhead discipline.

"Thou shalt keep and keep promptly all thy appointments with the school system. If thou art late or tardy or absent thou shalt provide a document of incontestable authenticity to prove that thou art not lying."

"In thy studies, a hundred per cent perfection is not demanded of thee, but thou shalt attain to within seventy-five per cent of perfection, or do the whole thing over."

It worked. I was never late because I hated to tiptoe into a hushed schoolroom, tardy. I tried to learn because I hated to admit in public that I didn't know the answer. I was afraid of cops and sheriffs and public embarrassment, but I wasn't above spitballs and dipping hair in inkwells. I had some manners but no morals. It was my general intention to do the things I liked to do and avoid the things I hated. My schooling proceeded on this precarious equilibrium between what I had to do and what I could get away with, and it was fairly successful.

After school the brakes on my behavior seemed to revert to a moral matter — my mother or father told me what I could or couldn't do and then left it more or less up to my conscience. Unfortunately at that age I didn't have one. All I had was the memory of a hairbrush and the promise of hell-fire, neither of which were wholly operative because I was something of a gambler and believed in my luck.

It was my custom at an early age to prowl the hillside back of our house in search of wild flowers and berries. The timber began only a little way from my back yard. It was jack pine and aspen, with little open parks of grass and wild flowers. Here and there an outcrop of limestone rock would make a miniature castle where wild rose bushes grew, and raspberries were to be found in season. In ever-widening circles I explored this side hill, and soon I was casting covetous eyes on White Rocks across the gulch.

This rocky prominence, however, belonged strictly to the other side of the gulch. To reach it I would have to cross Red Creek, a swift mountain stream which my parents considered dangerous for a child of my tender years. There was a standing order that my flower picking was to be done on my own side of the gulch. This made my side smaller, though in point of fact it embraced half the world. As a consequence I one day joined a group of older boys who were going over to the other side of the world.

The flowers were plentiful, and bearing a large bouquet I was returning over the plank across Red Creek when disaster overtook me. The current was swift and my eyes followed it off the plank. Before I knew it I was waist-deep in the water.

When I reached shore there was a high water mark on my overalls composed of dirty mill tailings. Any citizen of the town would know at a glance that I had been in Red Creek to the depth the mill tailings indicated. There was only one way out of my predicament — authorship.

Shrewdly I selected my grandmother for my first edition. I had, I said, been virtually kidnaped by some tough First Ward kids, abducted to the far side of the gulch, and had then been pushed into the creek. My grandmother, who mistook fiction for nonfiction, insisted that my father seek out the ruffians and turn them over to the law.

Shortly thereafter I found myself guiding my father toward the lurking place of some nonexistent kidnapers. As we approached the city limits my directions grew increasingly vague, and eventually it became necessary to confess that I might have been mistaken about the whole thing.

I had borne false witness against my neighbor, I had failed to honor my father and mother, but worst of all I had gotten my pants wet in a creek in which I might have drowned. My father took me behind a chokecherry bush and I yelled very loud indeed before he decided to stop.

"Will you ever do it again?" he demanded.

"No-o-o," I promised, "I won't do it ever again." And I didn't.

The next time I crossed Red Creek on that plank — and it was soon afterward — I crawled across it on my hands and knees, and if my soul was wrinkled, my pants were dry.

During my exile with my father in Florida and California, the hairbrush situation became inoperative because my father wasn't physically able to run me down and smite me, but the fear that I might be punished by his death restrained me somewhat.

When his death freed me of that restraint, another was waiting. There was a redheaded belligerent on our street in Deadwood who seemed to have been born my natural enemy. We were always colliding, and I was always backing down. I had seen him lick several other kids, and had been discouraged by the spectacle. I didn't so much dread the bloody nose as I did the aura of defeat. But the time was rapidly approaching when the aura of cowardice would become worse than that of defeat.

Our trouble originated from our first meeting, when "Fritz" was under the impression that I was a Rich Kid. When I first returned from California, the reporter on the daily paper had written an account of my father's death in which he had estimated the value of my inheritance. In doing so he had multiplied fifteen hundred and twenty acres by the wrong price per acre, arriving at a figure which made me a Rich Kid overnight. Fritz had no intention of letting a Rich Kid step on his toes, and had developed the habit of stepping on mine.

It was in January of 1917 that this matter came to a head. Together with a crowd of other boys we were sliding on Lincoln Avenue. We had made the trip down the street and had come to a stop beyond the Burlington tracks. As we started up the hill again, Fritz took up his favorite pastime.

"Stuck up!" he taunted me. "Just because your dad left you a pile of money you think you're smart."

"You're a liar!" I said hotly. "My dad didn't leave me a pile of money, and I ain't stuck up!"

"Did you call me a liar?" he asked ominously. "That's a name I don't take from anybody." He doubled his fist.

The pit of my stomach was cold, but I was more afraid

that public opinion would suspect me of being afraid than I was of impending violence. I restated my original assertion.

He pushed me.

I pushed him.

His fist banged against the side of my head. I doubled mine and tried to flatten his nose. I filled the air with my fists. Now and then one of my blows landed somewhere. If his landed on me, I didn't feel them.

Then the fight was interrupted. Mrs. White had observed the trouble from her window and had hastened out to stop it. She stepped between us.

My appetite for fighting had cooled, and my breath was coming in gasps. But because I welcomed the interruption of the fight, I felt morally obligated to continue it. I stepped around Mrs. White and took another swing at my opponent.

She collared me and swung me around. Her eyes were angry, so were mine — angry at the grasp on my collar. I couldn't hit her, but I could tell her.

"Go to hell!" I said. "Go to hell, you damned old Christian Scientist!"

The silence that fell upon my audience was sudden and complete. My opponent looked at me in awe. The little girls drew in their breath sharply. One of them said in tones of horror, "He swore! He swore at Mrs. White!"

Mrs. White's anger was now tinged with fear, the kind of fear that an adult feels when a group of small fry seems to be getting the upper hand. She retreated into the house to call the police.

This magic word gave wings to my heels. I didn't tarry.

Breathless, I reached the sanctuary of my own home and retired behind the front window curtains to watch for the arrival of the Law. After a time the sleds began to ply again, and I envied the carefree souls who were not fugitives from justice.

For twenty-four hours the blow failed to fall. My opponent, I later learned, had refused to divulge my name. But a little girl promptly supplied it.

The next afternoon, as I was sitting in the parlor reading a book, the phone rang. Aunt Ida answered it. The one-sided conversation which I overheard caused my heart to pound.

"Oh no!" said my aunt. "You must be mistaken! I'm sure that George would never have said anything like that!"

My digestive organs rearranged themselves violently. My heart thundered against my ribs. Forty lies crossed my mind, forty frantic revisions of what I had said to Mrs. White. None of them were good ones.

"George," said Aunt Ida, cupping her hand over the mouthpiece of the telephone, "did you swear at Mrs. White? Were you fighting in front of her house yesterday?"

"Me?" I asked. "Do you mean me? Well, yes, I had a little trouble, but it didn't amount to much."

"Did you swear at Mrs. White?"

"No!" I said indignantly. "Oh gosh no, I just told her to mind her own business was all. But maybe I swore at her a little. I can't remember."

My Aunt took her hand from the mouthpiece, and while she ate crow, I dined on even rougher fare, as I learned by eavesdropping that I was on my way down to apologize.

My journey down the hill to Mrs. White's house was not unobserved. All the kids stopped in their tracks to watch my aunt and me go by. She was the chariot, I was the captive barbarian. I wore a scowl to hide my shame.

"If you had called her anything else!" Aunt Ida said, criticizing my dialogue bitterly. "I don't see how I can hold my head up!"

I made no attempt to hold mine up. Staring at Mrs. White's shoelaces I said, "I'm sorry I cussed. I guess I was pretty mad when I said it."

The three of us smiled at one another from the teeth out, and I shook Mrs. White's hand as though it were a dead mackerel.

But once I had regained the street with my sled my progress became a march of triumph. For it was the consensus of public opinion that if Reefus and Fritz had been fighting in Mrs. White's yard, she would have had the right to stop them. But they were fighting in the street, and it wasn't her street, was it? Reefus did right in making her mind her own business.

A second fight was therefore needed to heal the vainglorious consequences of the first, and it was not long in coming. It arose out of the verbal battle that was raging on on both sides of the street concerning the Freedom of the Seas. The line of division was that of Democrat and Republican. The Democrats thought that Wilson was a statesman and the Republicans thought he was a mollycoddle. Right-thinking people shared the opinions of Teddy Roosevelt.

My opinion was correct, and those of opposite opinion were my personal enemies. Among the latter was a boy whose mother hadn't raised her boy to be a soldier. He was my enemy because he was keeping us out of war to the point where Kaiser Bill would be able to come over and conquer us.

One day when the war news was particularly bad, I was playing marbles with him on the school ground.

"We ought to be in there fighting right now," I said. "If Teddy Roosevelt was president we would be."

"Teddy Roosevelt is a jingo," the Pacifist said. "He'd like to get a lot of Americans killed so he could get some glory out of it."

"Teddy Roosevelt is no such a thing!" I shouted. "He had guts enough to fight for his country, and old Wilson never did!"

"Yeah," said the Pacifist, "and what did we get out of it? Just a bunch of no-good islands. Anyhow, what have we got to fight about?"

"The Freedom of the Seas," I replied. "They're sinking our boats, ain't they? It's just as much our ocean as it is theirs, ain't it?"

"We'd ought to keep our boats at home," he said unhappily.

"Hunh!" I snorted. "You're nothing but a goddam Pacifist!"

The Pacifist then hauled off and hit me in the eye.

As I went into the school building wearing the badge of my defeat, I was confused and disheartened by this turn of events. I was right and he was wrong. Yet he had won, and I had the black eye.

Even more confusing was the transition to high school. About the time the Germans were beginning their final big push, the school board handed me a diploma and dumped me out of the eighth grade. While the Germans were beginning their final retreat, I entered high school. My reactions to the new liberties of the high-school study hall were immediate. My eighth-grade teacher had been a tyrant who took nothing for granted. Possessing eyes like a falcon, she could diagnose the birth of a spitball at thirty paces and stare it down my gullet. She could also tell whether I was drawing a picture of Kaiser Bill in a book that was school property, or whether I was studying as directed. By comparison, my high-school teachers were complete dumbbells.

When the fear of my new surroundings had worn off, I looked around the study hall, feeling things out, appraising

the length of my rope. At the front of the hall on a platform a teacher sat at a desk, writing with a pen. How could
she tell whether I was studying or not? I decided that she
couldn't.

Pulling a rubber band from my pocket, I prepared a
missile, drew a bead on a classmate several rows away, and
whanged him back of the ear. He jumped. I bent virtuously
over my book, observing as I did so that the teacher hadn't
looked up from her task.

A spitball stung me viciously on the forehead.

Barricading myself behind my book, I went to work on
an arsenal.

In six weeks my arsenal included slingshots, blowguns,
and a box of stink bombs. The latter, dropping upon the
floor with a soundless tinkle, released a horrendous reek
which made the place practically uninhabitable. I fought
boredom with everything but books.

At the end of six weeks, the blow of retribution fell.

"What on earth has happened?" Aunt Ida demanded.
"Miss Cartwright sent home report cards that were covered
with A's. How dare you come home with a failure in
Algebra?"

I analyzed for her the weak and disagreeable traits of my
Algebra teacher, and bore down a little on the incompre-
hensible nature of the subject she was teaching. But it was
no go, neither Aunt Ida nor Uncle Harry seemed to have
any sympathy for the conditions I was facing.

I grew defiant. Whereupon Uncle Harry decided I needed a good licking. What followed was an inconclusive wrestling match from which I emerged with the suspicion that I had been the victor.

But there was small comfort in the victory. Uncle Harry's face was white and hard, and Aunt Ida regarded me with cold anger. Together they retired into their bedroom to hold a low-voiced consultation. Their voices came to me, ominous and disturbing. I sought the outdoors, feeling shaken.

The next morning I learned the verdict.

"George," said my aunt, "your uncle and I have decided that we can't educate you the way your father wanted us to. We're failing. So we're going to send you to a Military Academy where you'll have to behave yourself and study."

This invoked a picture which was not pleasant. It was a picture that differed little from the one I had read in the story about the German boy drafted by Kaiser Bill.

But my neck was stiff. I sat tight, hoping it would all blow over.

One day I came home from school to find literature from several military academies spread out on the table. There were a lot of smiling students pictured in these booklets, but for my money they were smiling from the teeth out. I felt like a calf in the branding corral, fighting and choking for air.

I looked at the rope and saw that it was strong. I looked at the word "freedom" and saw that it didn't mean anything of what it said.

"Hey!" I complained. "Don't get in such a hurry about this thing! Maybe my grades will get better."

Up to that point the difference between A and C on my report card wasn't enough to cause me any discomfort, but the difference between a military academy and the cabin I was building on the hill was enough to invite a more serious attention to Algebra. At the end of another six weeks my report card falsely accused me of being a good student. It wasn't so at all. I had simply discovered that conscience was a cash proposition.

One hundred dead sheep in a sheepshed were a cash proposition, and they were on my conscience because I had killed them. I had met a force that yelling wouldn't stop, for it had neither ears nor eyes. The Butte hadn't asked me to come there, and the Hills didn't care whether or not I stayed. But, just as my first spanking had been followed by a period of healing reconciliation, it was the Hills which now consoled my wounded pride.

The first Saturday after the roads cleared, I put a lunch and a Thermos jug into the car and headed for a spot as far away from the ranch as gasoline would carry me. Sunday would be a bad day on the trout streams and it was my intention to get far ahead of the procession of other fishermen by the time the sun rose the next morning. But as the road led me past the first good stream, my fishing hunger got the best of me. A deep pool was visible from the road and I couldn't resist it. As I set up my pole, my fingers were thumbs, my heart hammered with familiar excitement, and my steps hastened. At long last I had a line in the creek.

Nothing happened on the first cast, nor on the second. Then I saw that footprints had preceded mine. Someone was upstream ahead of me. I reeled in my line, and getting back into my car, headed farther into the hills in search of a ground-floor proposition.

An hour's driving brought me to the fork where a narrower road climbed more steeply into the hills. I followed the turns through the tunnel of trees, climbing all the way. As I reached the top the trees fell away and the road wound through barren slabs of rock. Then I dropped abruptly into the descent, the pines reappeared, then aspen and birch, and at last the spruce which signaled the approach to bigger water.

In the darkness, while my ears were filled with the unending murmur of the near-by stream, I slept fitfully, for the fishing fever was on me. At three o'clock I pulled on my rubber boots, slung on my creel, and set off down the railroad track to increase my lead on the Sunday trade.

In the dim hush of predawn my boots clumped awkwardly over the ties. The track arrowed straight down the canyon, but the sound of the stream frequently turned aside. For a time I would hear only the clumping of my boots, until the rush of water rejoined me again.

A bird twittered experimentally, suddenly a squirrel cut loose with his Tommy-gun chatter, and there was light. I could see a heavy mist rising from the water, and the brush was beaded with dew.

JUG BENEATH THE BOUGH

Baiting my hook I pushed in through dense willows toward the inviting depths of a beaver dam. As I moved cautiously in through the tender green brush, I suddenly saw a trout lying in the edge of the pool in shallow water. His size made my heart hammer — two pounds if he weighed an ounce!

Breathless, I studied the problem of placing my bait before his nose. Forlorn hope that I could cast through those willows without a snag. . . .

I backed carefully away, then crawling on hands and knees, I moved past him and reached the creek again below the dam. Carefully scaling the tangle of peeled logs on its face, I gained the top, examined my bait, stood erect and cast my line far back among the willows to my right.

The line began to move. There was an imperious yank and my pole bent sharply as the fish sought to regain the willows he had left. I horsed him out into the open water by main strength, but he would not come clear so I could see him. My line swirled powerfully about the pool as he lunged here and there in its depths. Then he broke water, only to plunge again. I got him to the surface and tried to reel in line, but I didn't have enough hands. Abandoning the crank on my reel I hauled in line with my left hand. At last, with a desperate heave compounded more of strength than of skill, I brained him on a tree far behind me on the bank.

An hour later, my basket was jammed with trout, and I

made my way back to the place where I had cached my lunch.

Carrying my lunch under one arm I found a spruce tree along the banks of the creek where a dense mat of needles lay beneath a network of boughs. I crawled in through the branches and sat down with my back against the tree. With the pungent odor of pine and spruce all around me, the sound of wind in the higher pines, the endless rolling of clear cold water at my feet, I ate my lunch and washed it down with hot coffee from a Thermos jug.

. . . Got my trout before sunrise . . . got all of the trout I could carry . . . my angle worms are gone and I've had e-nough to eat and nothing is bothering me. . . .

I slept.

Chapter VI

THE SWEAT OF MY FACE

TEN HOURS of uninterrupted sleep under a spruce tree cleared my head, and what snow and mud had bruised, spruce needles healed.

It wasn't hard to see just where I had made my mistakes. Perhaps I was lucky to have made so many of them the first year. My original intention still stood the test of intelligent inspection. There was nothing wrong with my thinking except that I hadn't thought far enough. Nothing had happened to my finances that a doubled bet and a good year wouldn't cure.

As I tooled the car down the mountain road, I saw that what I needed to recoup my losses was a cash crop. Hay wasn't a cash crop, at least not until it had been put through a band of sheep. Where my father had sold native hay at twenty dollars a ton, hay in the stack was now worth only three. If I mowed and stacked every acre of my hayland, I would still have less than a thousand dollars, gross. Planted in wheat or flax, the same land would return my investment thirty or forty fold. But wheat was falling in price —

101

there was too much wheat in the world. Flax then. Flax was scarce and the price was climbing. Every acre of flax, granted that 1927 should continue to be a wet year, could return fifty dollars an acre in cash. . . .

Less than two weeks after the flax was in the ground, I paid the last full measure of humiliation for my winter's mistakes — the shearers came.

Although the sheep had been grazing for more than a month on lush grass, many of them were old and all of them were thin as snakes. This alone would have made them hard to shear. But they had also slipped their wool because I had overfed them on grain. This meant that the wool had broken away from the pelt at the time of their foundering, and that the new wool had grown into the broken ends of the old growth. The result was a tangle of hard-cutting snarled wool, and the shearers hated me for it.

They had to stab their shears into the "cotted" areas and close the blades by main strength. If they tried to cut under the clump, they cut the sheep. If they cut over it, the shears could hardly be closed. The wool had to be sawed off in ragged cuts, and to the sheep it was less a shearing than a scalping. The sheep fought and kicked and wore the shearers down.

Consequently the job dragged on far beyond its normal time. The shearers complained about the pens, about the light, about shearing in July under a tin roof. They didn't like the drinking water. They didn't like me, or the profession of shearing sheep. At every opportunity they commented in raised voices that they had never in their lives seen such a goddam, ornery, kickin', fightin', sunzabitchin', goddam bunch of sheep!

My temper was also short. Up near the roof, where I was tamping wool, it was several degrees hotter than on the floor where the shearers were working. The weight I had lost during the winter had reduced the padding around my own nerves. The fact that I kept my mouth shut under these insults was not due to any righteous recognition of my own sins, but because this was the last shearing crew in the neighborhood, and I couldn't risk losing them.

On the third day the shearers approached the end of the task. They had left the bucks till the last, for bucks are hard to shear at best, and these of mine were of a breed which carries wrinkles from nose to tail. When the last ewe trotted out to rejoin the band, the hired man and I penned the bucks.

"Good God!" said one of the shearers. "Just look at them things! I ask you. . . ?" He made no move to catch one.

"Mister," he said at last, turning to me, "do you want them bucks sheared?"

"That's the general idea," I answered carefully.

"Do you want 'em sheared bad enough to pay a dollar a head?"

I recognized that this quadrupling of the agreed price was not a matter of money, but of intentional insult. But I kept my temper and reminded him of the original agreement.

"We didn't make no deal to shear fleece-grown sheep, neither," he countered. "Them *ewes* was worth two strings apiece, I could shear two good sheep easy in the time it took me to skin one of them knotheads."

I could say nothing. It was true.

Time passed.

They sheared the bucks.

When the shearers were gone and the last sack of wool dropped from the hanger the hired man looked inquiringly at me.

"What do we do now?" he asked.

It was a hard question to answer, for this was Saturday afternoon and it had been several weeks since I had gone fishing. But there was hay on the ground that should be raked and tomorrow it should be stacked. I had a right to lay off Saturday afternoon and Sunday because I was my own boss. But I knew by now that, although no pay checks changed hands, I had acquired a Boss.

"Catch two teams," I said to the hired man. "We'll both rake this afternoon."

2

The deep snow which had cursed me as a sheepman, blessed me as a farmer. It sank deep into the subsoil. It achieved a cool season that invited more rain. The moisture-laden clouds that swept up from the Gulf met cool air over my land, and what had so recently left the sea, poured again down the Missouri toward the sea. Springs flowed, trees prospered, and the grass was waist-high.

The wheat which had lain invisible beneath the big snow had sprouted there while the sheep died. Under the continuing rains it sent out many stalks. On every stalk there was a long head, and in the heads there were no kernels missing.

The flax plants stood stiffly in their orderly rows, and began to bloom in July. A square of sky blue appeared among the yellows and purples and greens of my bets upon land.

Once again, as in 1920, I was hounded by the task of harvesting the chips when the bets were paid. While rains interfered, an awareness of the value of hay pressed upon me from the other side. To rid myself of horses I bought a tractor sweep and hitched the tractor to the stacker to pull up each sweep load onto the stack. In doing so I was now free of the wreckage which horses had wrought. I was also free of the long slow trek to and from the field. At noon and at night we had only to cut the switch on the tractor and race home in the pickup at forty miles an hour where before we had plodded behind weary teams.

At the same time I had cut the stacking crew from three men to two. I was now both the sweep hand and the stacker team driver. In mowing I was a one-man show. With one foot on the tractor clutch and the other on the mower lift, with one hand on the steering wheel and the other on the rope that dumped the rake, I was completely and continuously employed.

Time was when the need to rest the horses had given me a chance to idle and smoke a cigarette, and every other round the horse mowers had to be oiled from an oil can. Now there was no need to stop, pressure grease guns and a tireless motor saw to that. I could, if I wished, run the tractor twenty-four hours a day.

My machinery was better and it accomplished more, but my tasks were multiplied. While the sheep still had to be herded every day of their lives, increased bets upon land made bigger crews necessary, and the absence of enough good labor pressed continually on all of my operations. Meanwhile Dakota went on tearing leaves from the calendar, one day at a time. . . .

. . . While hay was still in the windrow, the oats were getting ripe . . .

. . . while shocking oats, the wheat got ripe . . .

. . . it was time to bind the flax . . .

. . . The bucks had to be cut out of the band and shut up to prevent another January lambing. In a jangle at the chutes the herder quit, and I had to herd sheep for two days while Uncle Harry searched for another man. . . .

. . . The threshing machine had started its run on a nearby ranch, and if I wanted neighbors to come with their bundle wagons to help me harvest my grain, I would now have to go with a bundle wagon to help them on theirs. . . .

. . . While we threshed nine days in my fields, I hauled

grain home through wild hay meadows that would soon be past their prime. . . .

Like the mythical greedy one, who had placed one coin too many in the sack, some of my sacks burst their seams and spilled the coins upon the ground. Yet, I recouped my winter's loss. The farmer earned more than the sheepman had lost.

My sweat was not begrudged by me, nor was my labor slavery. A dozen times a day I looked up to see evidence of accomplishment, to admire a hayfield populous with rainproof stacks, to congratulate myself for a grain field dappled with shocks. And from one task I was drawn by appetite to another, and the new task was one that I wanted to accomplish as badly as I had wanted to catch that big trout.

But my own attitude toward these tasks was not shared by transient labor. The ground swell was gathering under the stock market boom. Higher and higher wages, shorter and shorter hours were making farm work less and less attractive to men looking for jobs. The pool halls were filled with idle men whose time hung heavy on their hands. Yet, fishing for a hired man in these murky depths was like fishing for suckers — there were many nibbles but no strikes. "How many cows do I have to milk?" one prospect would ask. "Will I have to work in the stack?" another would inquire. Sweat was needed but sweat was reluctant, and it came high.

I hired a dope addict who lasted one day. As a pharmacist's mate just out of the Navy, he had sampled forbidden drugs and had acquired an appetite which no rancher could satisfy. I hired an Indian by the name of Charlie. He was a full-blooded Sioux, young and strong, but with no enthusiasm stirring behind his dark, agate eyes. I put him to greasing the fittings on the tractor. He began with those he could reach lying down. With an effort he reached those which permitted a sitting posture. When I looked up from my own task to see how he was getting along, I saw him on the sky line, heading back for town.

The only answer to this kind of labor market was more and better machinery. It was never hard to find a man to ride a tractor seat, but it was always hard to find one willing to stoop for bundles under a hot sun, or maul hay around on the top of a haystack with a pitchfork.

My acreage did not justify the purchase of a big combine which would bind and thresh in one operation. I could only work toward this solution by using the Farmall on more acres for longer hours.

One task led into another, one need gave birth to another. As Next Year became this year, this year became Next Year again. My acreages increased, my line of machinery lengthened, and the sweat of my face was not diminished.

. . . 1928 . . .

. . . 1929 . . .

3

The prairie sod was a patient, persistent force. Vigilantly it watched its chance to reclaim the conquests my plow had made. At every spot where the plow had been thrown out of the ground by a rock, wherever there was the slightest flaw in my plowing, wheat grass lifted its tall stalks and placidly went to seed. At every point where the wiry roots of "nigger wool" had been too much for the power of my tractor, an island of buffalo grass sent out its trailing shoots and doggedly went about the task of repossessing its own. In the low-lying sloughs the wiry, unpalatable stalks of salt grass fought me doggedly, and even on the most faultless of plowing, survived with a persistence worthy of a better cause.

I saw that if I hoped to hold in check the acreage which my eyes now claimed, I would have to leave off breaking sod and plow my old fields. This task I knew would be too much for my spindle-legged all-purpose tractor, so I bought one that was not spindle-legged.

It was a hulking brute that purred and growled and put its back into the job. It plowed deeply enough to lunge beneath the rocks, it had the power to bull through the toughest nigger wool. It had one further virtue, it possessed lights, and by virtue of that possession it became completely tireless.

The hired man could take it over at dawn, bringing fuel and grease and plow lays. He could plow while I did chores and slept. When I came out at noon, the tractor would puff idly while I filled its tanks, and it would plow tirelessly again until the hired man had returned from his hour of rest. When I had milked and eaten supper, the tractor would wait patiently, still running coolly and smoothly, while I changed the lays again in the last light of the sun. Then, with its lights peering steadily ahead and behind, it would lunge on into the dark.

One night, when my legs grew cramped and tired, I wired the steering wheel to the fender, and while the furrow wheel kept its place on the land, I walked off a dozen paces to see that thing at work.

Casting one eye ahead upon the prairie sod, the other behind upon the broad pencil line of black, its motor thrumming with the tones of its power, the machine marched on through the night, so intent upon its task of growing food upon virgin prairie sod that it hadn't missed my presence at the wheel.

I thought, It's growing loaves of bread and juicy steaks and paint for unpainted houses to protect them from the sun. . . .

The tractor was getting too far ahead of me. I raced after it, caught it, and climbed aboard.

4

In the fall of 1929, when the stock market achieved its spectacular autumnal moulting, and the leaves of common stock came fluttering down, flax was still three dollars a bushel, and lambs were eleven cents. Between them, my flax check and my lamb check gave me an affluence which seemed to justify a vacation in the East.

The nature of the vacation was determined to some extent by the fact that at twenty-five I was still unmarried. My private life had been jostled from time to time by the ups and downs of my academic career. The girl who had placed me in peril of Mechanical Drawing had, almost at once, shown a preference for a senior student in metallurgy, and my feeling for a telephone operator whom I had met in my junior year in college was more a gesture than an emotion. Graduation severed the tie and I returned to the life of my own countryside to find that I was out of context.

Classmates in high school had wedded or departed, the new crop was involved in its own invisible ties, and I was a sun-blistered rancher too much engrossed in his work for months at a time to carry on anything but a desultory dating of transient acquaintances.

At twenty-five I felt the lack of companionship. Living in a home kept in a state of cleanliness and repair by my aunt and uncle, well fed and darned, I still felt this lack. The world was paired off, two and two, but I was still walking in single file. Far more than I imagined, my trip East was motivated by the hope that lightning would strike.

It wasn't lightning that struck, but a sense of contentment and well-being that vanished with desolating abruptness when I came away from the girl who had invoked it. That this feeling had been fully shared, I learned from a letter which awaited me on my return.

Something had to be done, but would the ranch let me do it? There would have to be two homes, and there would have to be income for both homes. Before any of that could happen, it seemed only decent that there should be something in the way of a face-to-face courtship. But Dakota had no concern about anyone who lived beyond the boundaries of Dakota. The blizzards came and went, and the men came and went. The sheep had to eat, and I had to be there.

By spring I was thoroughly tired of being pushed around by my land at a time which I felt was crucial to my happiness. I resolved to bring matters to a head, and I revised my acreages of farming sharply upward. I was going to make room for two homes and two incomes on a Dakota ranch.

I worked the hired men and they worked me. A tractor only paid off when it was in motion, and I did all the chores alone so that the hired men could start the tractors at dawn. I cleaned all the seed so that the small tractor and grain drill would never have to stop.

The chores I performed at a gallop so that I could clean the seed before the sacks in the field were emptied into the ground. The fanning mill jigged and whirred and sifted wild buckwheat and sunflower seed from the flax.

It threw the dust into the air, the chaff into a pile, and the clean seed into a hopper from which I scooped it into sacks. I set my arm in motion and kept it at work until the mill hopper emptied and had to be refilled. It was work. But it had an end in view and I had no quarrel with it. At ten o'clock I would hasten out with the seed I had cleaned, arriving as likely as not just in the nick of time. I would help the hired man fill his drill, I would stack the sacks against the line of his work, and go over to the other tractor to fill and replenish its tanks while the hired man took the car in to the house and ate an early dinner. I would plow until he returned. . . .

The Federal Farm Board was already calling the thing that I was doing "Blind Greed". But to me it was a labor of love.

Chapter VII

THORNS AND THISTLES

To A FIELD OF WHEAT, just ready to branch out from the first thin shoots, the right kind of rain cloud could spell the difference between three bushels to the acre and thirty. On the other side of the picture, the wrong kind of rain cloud could transform a spring lambing season into a chaotic shambles. The same rain could do both these things.

To me, half rancher, and half farmer, every rain cloud had been both a blessing and a curse. The rain that caused my wheat to head well, might spoil hay in the windrow. The early spring rains, so necessary to a good hay year, could lop ten per cent off my lambing percentage. I looked at every rain cloud therefore with mixed emotions, and cast my vote according to the role that was uppermost in my mind at the moment. While I recognized that rains were not achieved by such balloting, I couldn't escape the feeling that they were somehow under the influence of my will.

In the spring of 1930 rain had not persecuted the sheepman, but I fully expected that wet fields would persecute the farmer. For good and sufficient reason, I was planting five hundred acres, and to get the job done in time I would have to keep the tractors rolling.

No rain fell through April, and we circled our fields steadily, without interruption. On the first of May the end of the farming was in sight. I was pulling a drill with the small tractor, planting the last patch.

The rain cloud which peered over my shoulder from the northern sky line was therefore no friend of mine. I eyed the tall, high-piled masses as I worked, suspecting that I was about to be chased by them. I wanted to finish. *Then* I would take the rain.

The cloud went away.

Two weeks later when a rain cloud appeared on the sky line to the west of the Butte, I was harrowing the same field, but I wasn't pushing the cloud away. I was willing it to come nearer and wash me off the tractor like a drowned rat.

The cloud went away.

Weeks passed and I watched my flax dwindle with a sinking heart.

Rain had fallen now and then, but it had been stingy. The clouds came up slowly, the rain did not pound on the roof, it only pattered. It wet the surface of the ground, but one's fingers could rake the mud aside and reach dust.

The wheat, because it was thin on the ground, held its own for a time. I knew it couldn't become a bumper crop, but it could still make a profitable yield. The flax was dwindling more rapidly, but in my opinion still had a chance.

By the Fourth of July the prospect was desperate. I was herding sheep that day, the herder having laid off to do his patriotic duty with a whiskey bottle. As I saddled the horse to go out with the sheep, two highly unscientific thoughts crossed my mind: it always rains on the Fourth of July, it always rains when you leave your slicker at home.

The theory was that it rained when people didn't want it to. One layer of my mind said, "Ridiculous!" The other looked at the fields and said, "You need rain. Don't leave any stone unturned to get a rain. Leave your slicker at home. It will rain then, because you don't want it to."

I left my slicker at home.

About noon, the clouds came up west of the Butte. It was a line storm, black and dense and alive with the slashing fire of lightning. The booming thunder was a cheering sound that bore the certainty of rain. The thought crossed my mind that I should return to the barn posthaste for my slicker, but I relished too much the thought of getting wet. The air was sweet with the smell of approaching rain, and I wouldn't lift a finger that might push it away. I watched the cloud sweep nearer with bated breath.

Then a south wind sprang up at my back, vigorous with a will of its own. As it tore at my hat and jumper I looked toward the source of that enemy wind and cursed it as

116

though it were a human being. As I watched, the sweep of the cloud was halted. It hung there for a time, giving rain to my neighbors on the north, then it swung slowly eastward and passed on down the creek bottom, beyond my reach.

I cursed the enemy wind, I cursed the cloud, I cursed the goddam country that I had chosen for a place to live.

When my rage had worn itself out, I was disturbed. My voice hadn't been that of a reasoning, educated man. It had been the hoarse, irrational bellowing of a wounded caveman. I knew that the earth was a round ball of matter, whirling by physical laws, and that its weather moved on the same terms. I knew that rain, or the lack of it, was ruled by cause and effect that reached off somewhere toward the North Pole and beyond. I, a college man who knew these things, had been using a slicker as a primitive charm, and when it failed I had torn at this hostile force with my vocal chords, like a prisoner trying to dig his way through stone walls with his fingernails. It was irrational, but I couldn't escape the feeling that somehow I could bend this force to do my will. The cave man was slow to learn that he could only duck.

The next day, after a brief mental struggle at the barn door, Dakota again sent me forth to herd sheep without a slicker. And again no rain fell.

I had to have a crop from Dakota.

I didn't get it.

Grimly then I set about the task of salvaging the meager

products that the year had provided. My binder found a six-bushel yield of wheat and only enough flax to fill the seed sacks that I had carried to the field to plant. At the same time the price of these diminished yields was sharply lower. Prosperity was disappearing around corners.

It was no time to marry. Added to the fact that my occupation was cursed by Surplus, my own acres were cursed by Famine. The wheat I had grown wouldn't have kept a bakery running a week, yet the price of wheat went lower.

I couldn't do anything about the Farm Board, I couldn't do anything about the rain. But the rain, and the Farm Board, were blind and I had eyes.

My sheep were not suffering from famine, nor were they likely to. Russian thistles had taken over the stubble fields and thrived upon the drought. In their early stages they were a fernlike growth with young and tender stems. As they matured they took on the ball-like shape by which they reseeded themselves, rolling across country in the winter winds. Bristly and unpalatable in their late stages, there was a stage in which they could be made into good hay. This stage was brief, but the tractor mower was equal to the task. In one week I cut and raked more than a hundred tons of good Russian thistle hay. With my hold-over from the year before, I had plenty of hay, and I kept all of my ewe lambs.

That fall a Dakota sheepman's fancy grimly turned to thoughts of love.

Chapter VIII

THE CITY OF DREADFUL NIGHT

THE PROBLEM of winter herding was less exacting on one's skill than upon one's ability to withstand long hours of watching the band in the cold. To keep the sheep in sight, on one's land, and off the neighbors', and to keep the coyotes away, was all that the job called for. The sheep could have been confined in a corral and fed hay throughout the winter, but no South Dakota sheepman's hay budget could withstand such heavy consumption, and the plain fact was that the sheep thrived better on pasture than on hay.

The endless leisure was my worst enemy. I could only fill it with reading. The reading of current magazines, I found, was not an unmixed blessing. For the most part the stories dealt with love and courtship. This was unfortunate, for in any comparison between the fiction characters and myself, I always came off second best. These heroes always seemed to conquer their frustrations. I couldn't seem to make any headway against mine. My initiative in these matters did not appear in a favorable light.

Nor did the quality of my love. In the stories the lovers thought of nothing but one another. I frequently thought about Russian thistles, coyotes, fishing, and surplus. Sometimes the image of the girl I supposedly loved could not be sharply recalled. Perhaps my love was not love at all, but something my mind had manufactured from its own necessities and loneliness.

Throughout the winter I walked the treadmill of my own footprints, cheerful when the letters came, gloomy when they were slow in coming. I walked thus, head bent, hands clasped behind my back, until one day I saw the first shoot of the new year's grass. I looked at the cloudless sky, and at my neighbors busily burning trash in preparation for planting. "O. K.," I said grudgingly, "I'll bury some seed, but I'll never count on anything but sheep again."

It was a new lambing situation that I had to face that spring. Up to that time I had lambed in the winter, preferring to risk blizzard in order to lamb in dry sheds, free from the mud and hazards of the Dakota spring. But winter lambing required good hay and lots of it. So I had chosen to lamb in milder weather on prairie grass.

Range sheepmen had been doing it for several thousand years, and sheep — when they were running their own business, without the help of humankind — had doubtless done it that way for twice ten thousand years. It was the natural way, and the cheapest from the standpoint of feed, though it cost more in labor. For lambing operations are based on one dominant principle — to avoid banding too many ewes and young lambs in one place.

120

Range sheepmen habitually hire a man to handle each day's drop. With lambs coming at the rate of a hundred and fifty a day, the night drop is held by a herder when the hand moves on, the day drop by another, and the following day the two drops are combined and the men thus freed go back to take over the next twenty-four hours' lambing. The more haste in combining the drops, the greater the loss in disowned lambs. Lambing technique is a rough compromise between what should be done, and what can be done.

I couldn't hire nine men, so I made my plans accordingly. I bought lambing tents to handle the new lambs on the prairie in bad weather, and I put a rack on my pickup to haul them into the corrals. There, I could use fencing and hay, rather than men, to hold the drops apart long enough for the lambs to become acquainted with their mothers.

We didn't need the lambing tents that spring; the weather was as hot and balmy in May as it had normally been in July. There was grass on the wild hay meadows which had not been cut the summer before, but elsewhere the grass crop was thin. I lambed on my hay meadows under a blazing sun, there were no chilled lambs, there was no haste in picking them up, no hurry at all — except for rain.

But the job was still not easy. Each ewe had to be caught. It was my custom to pick up the lamb and try to entice the ewe within grabbing distance. Driven by her attachment for the lamb she would edge cautiously closer. I held the lamb with increasing nervousness, knowing that if I missed the first grab at the ewe, the ensuing chase might be a long one. At the proper moment I grabbed for her topknot and tossed her into the pickup.

When I had a load I drove in to the barn, stenciled a number on ewe and lamb with black paint, and put each pair into an individual pen. The barn corners were all filled with them wherever a panel could be set against the wall. I had forty or fifty of these private wards in operation all the time. Water had to be carried to them in pails and the ewes had to be fed hay twice a day. Sometimes a wool-blind ewe had to be sheared, sometimes a lamb who hadn't found the teat himself would have to be fed. They all had to be watched and their progress appraised. When the twenty-four-hour stretch was up, the pens had to be emptied into the larger drop corrals.

There were a thousand details to be looked after, and all of them under the steady pressure from the lambs which were arriving all the time. I was a doctor, a nurse, an ambulance driver, a cook, a dietician juggling trays, I was a male nurse who strong-armed the unreasonable patients, and I was the charwoman who swamped out at night while the rest of the staff slept.

When the twenty-one days were over, we sharpened our knives and relieved the lambs of their tails. The tail count indicated that we had lambed ninety-eight per cent, and the herder took my best lamb crop to date out into the south section for their summer range.

By late June I had given up hope that any crop would grow on the acreage planted to small grain. I made up my mind to cut it for hay. As for the flax fields, they wouldn't even make hay and I planned to use them for the sheep.

The herder complained about the grass on the south section.

"It's blowing up," he said. "The sheep won't do nothing but run, and they ain't doing any good on it."

"All right," I said, "take them north and hold them on the flax fields. But keep them off the wheat — I want to cut that for hay."

Four days later he approached me again.

"The lambs are scouring on that flax," he said. "It ain't doing them no good."

I looked at them and they looked rough.

"Put 'em on the wheat," I said. "That flax seems to be bad medicine."

"The water holes are blowing up," he said to me next. "The first sheep there muddies the water and the rest won't drink."

I looked at the spring-fed water holes and saw that they were stagnant, that when riled they turned black with the sediments of blue shale.

"All right," I said, "we'll corral at night and hold them on water at the wells."

That night after supper I started the engine and pumped the well for an hour before the last sheep walked away from the tank.

The next day a forest fire broke out in the Black Hills to the west. The smoke climbed to a tremendous height and poured south along the hills. Before night five more "smokes" had appeared on the sky line, reddening the night sky, as seventy-five thousand acres of timber blazed.

That night my well coughed and spit blue mud. It was dry.

The following morning, while a pall of acrid smoke concealed the countryside, I went to town and bought a wagon tank to fit my truck, and began to truck water eight miles from city mains.

The Dust Bowl had begun. All over the Great Plains disgruntled men, beaten down by bad wheat prices and bad crops, cursed the tractor and the plow. The tractor, they said, had made the surplus, and the plow had made the Dust Bowl. But for me the Dust Bowl began the day my wells went dry, and when seventy-five thousand acres of virgin timber burst into flames because they too were dry.

The lambs that I trailed to the railhead in October bore the unmistakable signs of Famine. They were potbellied, their wool was fuzzy and dull, and they were ten pounds a head too light. Their mothers had walked too far for dry, bulky grass, and had waited too long at the troughs for too little water. Upon their hindquarters, the lambs wore the rattling dungballs that were the souvenir of my experiment in grazing flax fields. In the tail end of the band walked the "little dogs," the peewees that had been weaned in early summer by the drought and had ever since been rustling for themselves. Behind the "little dogs" I walked, far from proud to call any of them mine.

THE CITY OF DREADFUL NIGHT

It was a poor time to take Famine to market, for Surplus was taller than it had been the fall before. There was too much wheat, too much meat, there were too many acres of farmed land. Government was trying to do something about it. The Farm Board had been appointed and its chairman had already hurled diatribes at the farmers, whom he accused of being guilty of Blind Greed. Others were saying the Tractor had caused it, that the only thing which would save us would be to go back to the horse.

At the same time long bread lines in the cities seemed to indicate that there was no lack of appetite for steaks and bread. Surplus existed only in the market place, not in the streets. While bread and steaks went begging, beggars went without steaks and bread; and while the lambs one trailed to market were the children of Famine, at market they would become Surplus, when, having been translated into terms of money, they would become Famine again. All of which seemed utterly insane and depressed me no end.

I loaded my lambs on the cars and billed them out for Chicago, with the privilege of selling them in Sioux City en route.

I boarded the caboose. It was empty. Always before the caboose had been full. Ranchers have little time to sow wild oats, but the shipping season has always been the season in which to do it. The terminal market towns had long made a good thing of these annual binges. Taxis met the incoming trains to tout for sporting houses and gambling dives, bellhops did a land office business in bootleg liquor and the "girls on call" fluttered in and out of the hotels, their stockings well-lined with five and ten-dollar bills.

But wild oats don't grow in Dust Bowls. I was alone on the way car and I was not going because I wanted to sow wild oats, but because I was ready to sow tame ones. I was going to Chicago to marry a girl.

I was out of debt. The stocks my father had left me were gold stocks, a commodity which thrived upon money panics and Surplus. Gold stocks had reached a point on the market at which they could put me out of debt. I sold them.

Now my eggs were all in one basket. The sheep were all mine, the land was mine, and every cent that came to me in income would be mine. The lamb check from my two carloads of lambs would see me through the winter. The wool check from my band of ewes would carry me through the summer, and into better times. I was through waiting.

There was no one on the car but the train crew, and they were cussing President Hoover.

At two A.M. we reached the end of the division. I lost my caboose and acquired another one. The new conductor worked dourly on his train sheet and the new brakie dosed himself earnestly with aspirin. As daylight filtered in through the windows, the conductor pointed to the fields through which we were passing.

"They had grasshoppers through here," he said.

I had heard about grasshoppers and looked out the window with morbid interest. There was nothing to see but

126

bare ground and sickly stalks of corn, leafless and forlorn. Nothing at all spectacular.

At the next stop a shipper got on.

"I hear you've had grasshoppers around here," I said.

"I'll say we've had 'em," he replied.

"What do you do about them?" I asked. "Can you poison them, or what?"

"There ain't anything to do about them," he said hopelessly. "I tried poison, and you might as well try to dry up the ocean. You hear a lot of talk about controlling grasshoppers, but there ain't no way to control 'em. I put up Russian thistles for hay and that's what I'm wintering on. Hoppers don't seem to like thistles and I don't blame 'em."

Conversation lagged. We stared out of the window as the land poured by, each of us lost in his own brand of self-sympathy.

In Sioux City my lambs were penned in an outside pen because they hadn't been consigned to any commission firm in that city. While I was going through the pen to check on their feed and water, a commission man came by and made an effort to get the job of selling them.

He went away and after a time came back with a buyer.

The buyer looked dourly at the lambs. When the commission man mentioned a price of five dollars and twenty-five cents per hundred pounds, the buyer started to walk away.

"I took a beating on some of that droughty stuff last year. I don't want 'em. But if you want to throw out twenty per cent of them at four cents I'll take the rest from you at five."

That wasn't enough money. I was sure I could do better in Chicago.

That night I boarded another empty caboose. The conductor worked on his train sheet, the brakeman made coffee. Until the train left the yards the two men paid no attention to me. But, as the train gathered speed I felt their eyes following me whenever I stood up to stretch or move about the car.

"Better not stand up any more than you can help," one of them said finally. "This is a hot-shot freight and you're liable to go through the end of the car if the engineer throws his air. If you don't believe this is a fast train, take a look at the bo's climbing off when we get to Manilla."

At Manilla I saw fourteen bums climb off the train and slouch away. A fifteenth stuck it out on top of the car ahead of the caboose. At the next stop the conductor brought him inside, and the brakie gave him a cup of coffee.

The man was shivering. His clothes were the clothes of Famine. His eyes were red-rimmed and dazed with something more than cold. When I tried to strike up a conversation he had nothing but monosyllables. He sat hunched in his shabby overcoat, ignoring the land which poured by the window.

"Where are you going?" I asked him.

"Back up the line," he replied, and shrugged deeper into his overcoat.

He left the train at Savannah.

The lambs reached the Chicago yards at noon and disappeared into the maw of the world's largest market. I wandered through a tangled maze of shabby, unpainted pens and scales and inclined runways. At last I found the pen which held my shipment. The commission man was going over them.

"These your lambs?" he asked me.

I admitted it.

"They got here too late for today's market," he said. "We may have trouble with this bunch of lambs."

I couldn't defend them. "Get a fill on them," I said, "they've come a long way."

In the morning I saw that the commission man had kept his word, the lambs were full. But the the sale barn was empty of buyers. With the exception of a crew feeding hay, I was the only man in the shed.

The commission man put in an appearance in midmorning.

"Market is slow today," he said. "Come back later."

I did. He hadn't found a buyer, but he had put in a call for a Michigan buyer who sometimes "takes a flyer in this kind of stuff."

When I returned again it was in time to see a handler hazing the little dogs off down a lane to the scales, their dungballs rattling like a band of Sioux Indians heading for a powwow.

"I sold 'em!" the commission man exulted with an air of achievement.

"How much?" I asked.

"Four cents," he replied.

Pocketing a check for five hundred and sixty dollars, a check which represented the return on twelve months' work with eight hundred ewes, I left the realm of Surplus and went out into the streets of a city where men were hungry and sleeping in doorways.

An elevated carried me to the suburb where I had planned to talk about marriage. I entered a home that had been furnished during the stock market boom. There were deep carpets, colorful drapes, and mellow lighting. I felt out of place in it. The sun-tanned face I saw in the mirror over the mantel as usual looked out of place above a white collar; and my lamb check wouldn't have carpeted this house.

There were quite a few people in the room. All of them were strangers, including the girl I had thought I wanted to marry. If my face was too dark, theirs were too white, and their hands too soft. Everyone was complaining because someone didn't do something about Business.

It had never crossed my mind up to that time that anyone should do anything for me. My quarrel had been a personal affair between myself and the weather. These men didn't know anything about weather.

Before I knew what was happening I heard my own voice delivering a lecture. It was a geology lecture and the gist of it was that weather was in back of the whole thing. I told them that people shut themselves up in cities and forgot that weather was the thing that made business or broke it. Business was sick, I said, because weather was sick. And weather wasn't sick because people had plowed or stopped using horses, but because something had changed its mind over the other side of the North Pole.

Nothing was changed by my sermon. I had convinced myself, not them. In a parlor a thousand miles from home I had seen that the only thing I could do about weather was learn to duck. It was worth knowing.

My courtship came to nothing. The girl was a stranger. My love for her had been manufactured out of some ingredient that no longer flowed through my veins. A dozen times her bland ignorance of what I considered to be realities annoyed and irritated me. She had a religion. I didn't. She didn't like Herbert Hoover. I did.

The whole thing began to look like a bear trap. But she was slow in realizing that I had graduated.

"You're smoking too much," she said. "When we're married I'm going to cut down on your tobacco."

Later she said, "You've been working too hard, that ranch will ruin your health. When we're married you can find something better to do with that brain of yours. . . ."

"We're not going to be married," I said. "I'm not built for it. I'm sorry, but that's the way it is."

As I took the elevated back to the stockyards, I was never in my life more desolately alone. Not only had I renounced love that was freely offered, but I had come to doubt my own capacity for ever loving anyone. There was dust in my thinking machinery, and dull hatred deep in my heart.

I boarded the train for home. It was empty. Famine doesn't travel, nor Surplus. Both stay at home.

Before the train pulled out two men got on. One of them, obviously a trainman riding on a pass, retired under his cap and went to sleep. The other joined me in the smoker.

"My God," he said, "what's the matter up here? Is everybody dead? Since I got on the train at New Orleans there's been nothing to do but match pennies with the porter."

"It's the Depression," I said. "Everybody is staying home."

"I've been hearing about it," he said.

"Where have you been that you had to hear about the Depression?" I wanted to know.

"Chile," he replied. "Working in a copper refinery. But they don't call it the Depression down there — they call it the God Damned Gringoes. We're getting the blame for it. It's getting so an American has to have a bodyguard to walk down the street for a beer. I've been jumped on from behind, and spit on in a crowd. They think we're gypping them on the price of copper."

So everybody in the world hated everyone else. Why? Had Surplus made Famine, or was Famine making Surplus? The engineer and I gnawed long upon the subject, but we got nowhere. He went to his berth and I went to mine.

I lay in my bunk awake, groveling at the humiliation of taking droughty lambs to market and bringing home a check that wouldn't pay the herder his summer's wages. I was shamed too by the fool who had thought he was in love.

I turned out the light and closed my eyes upon these thoughts, but they continued under my lids. I couldn't sleep.

I turned on the light and read. As I turned a page a dollar sign leaped out of the type into my attention. *Scribner's Magazine* was offering two thousand dollars for the winner of a prize contest for a long short story.

Two thousand dollars was a handsome sum, and at home I had a stack of manuscript that I had worked on from time to time during the long winter evenings. It was a story about a Dakotan.

Dakota had kicked me around and deprived me of all the things that I wanted. Perhaps now it would permit me to sell a piece of that experience for $2000?

Uncle Harry and Aunt Ida met me at the station expecting a returning bridegroom. Instead they met an absentminded author who was writing a story in his head.

Chapter IX

BRICKS WITHOUT STRAW

MY GRANDFATHER had died two years after I was born, but I knew him better than I knew my own father because Uncle Harry had passed on to me a word-of-mouth record of his goings and comings. These were in the form of anecdotes, endlessly repeated. Many of them were funny, but when I had long since memorized them and had ceased to laugh, I had perceived implications in them that revealed a man who was in deadly earnest. There was something he wanted that brought him from Plymouth, England to Deadwood Gulch. To gain it he had risked his life in war, and braved the danger of death at the hands of the Sioux. The thing he wanted, the thing that had destroyed his capacity for contentment, was the same thing that had sent me home from school with a college diploma to face an antagonist that I knew full well was tough. I was too close to my own story to see it or tell it, but I thought I could tell his, and I knew how I wanted to tell it.

134

Contemporary authors in the 20's and 30's refused to grant their characters the dignity of any intelligent compulsion. They seemed to prefer greed and sex and Freudian complexities as the mainsprings of human life. It was an era of the sordid and unhappy ending. Every author who had earned critical acclaim had pitied and patronized his characters.

I thought I had my hands on something new and true. If I could turn into fiction the compulsion that had prompted my grandfather's restless energy, and fix it upon paper in the same light that his son recalled and admired him, then my story could very well become a grandson who would continue my name.

It was two thousand dollars that attracted me to the quest, but it was a continuation of my grandfather's restlessness that so powerfully engrossed me in the task.

Through the haze of an upstairs bedroom filled with fumes of countless cigarettes, I sought the goal which drove and led me to gamble for big winnings. While the cigarette butts ringed my desk top in the pattern of a bear-claw necklace, and discolored coffee cups sat around in the clutter of papers which my disorderly haste had wrought, I struggled toward a solution.

If I was placing in my grandfather's mouth the opinions that I had expressed in a Chicago parlor, they were opinions which he would have endorsed; and while my flight from the demands of marriage did not necessarily prove anything but my own weakness, his life demonstrated clearly that there was something compelling him that was more powerful than love for home or a family. Possessing both, he still pursued the other thing. Many times he acquired sums that would have housed and clothed them all on a grander scale, but each time he had preferred to sink the money in a new tunnel in a new hill. What did he seek in the hill that was not money and not happiness? I thought that he was seeking a success that would give some lasting significance to his name.

As time passed, and the contest deadline approached, I pursued what I was convinced was the answer, and attempted to capture it in words. I devoted less and less time to sleep; I was more and more impatient of interruption. Sentences fled before me down the dim corridors of my mind. I limped along after them as best I could.

On one occasion I let the fire go out and was conscious of being cold. I picked up the scuttle to put coal in the stove and found it empty. I went out to get coal, seeing as I did so, events which I had never witnessed in a decade in which I had not yet been born. I was recalled to my own decade by the discovery that I had gone down the hill to the well and had hung the coal scuttle on the pump.

When the story was finished I thought that my words had captured what my imagination had seen. I thought the answer was there on the page.

But if I had found an answer, it was an old answer to an old question that Dakota had asked a man long ago. Outside my window Dakota was asking an immediate question that demanded an immediate answer: "Are you going to plant?"

To do anything about 1932 I would have to have some money. I didn't owe anyone and I owned my sheep, but 1932 was not a year in which sheep and machinery and land could be borrowed on at a bank. No banker felt any confidence that he would ever see his money again, and most certainly he didn't want sheep or machinery or land. A few banks had tried to foreclose and take over such security, but farmers had conspired to make the foreclosure sales a mockery. Someone bid one dollar on the land. As the auctioneer labored for a higher bid, the farmers stood grimly silent with clenched fists and there were no more bids. The banker received the dollar.

Banks had quit lending money. Only the government dared lend money.

Two government agencies were available for such loans. There was a seed loan which could be obtained from a government agency by signing an application blank and mortgaging the crop. For stockmen, there was the Regional Agricultural Credit Corporation which was willing to lend money on livestock.

To plant that year I asked for, and obtained, five hundred dollars. As the planting season progressed, tractor breakdowns and machinery repairs bit into this sum. I still expected the arrival of a check from the story I had written, if not the prize. It seemed to me no more than fair that the author should be able to provide the funds for planting that other four hundred acres. But the post-office box yielded nothing but circulars, and as lambing time approached I put my last dollar in the ground. My planting added up to one hundred acres.

It would soon be time to lamb. The sheep were there, good Dakota sheep, bred to Dakota bucks, and ready to lamb on good Dakota grass. The only thing that was lacking was money. Money was not and never had been a matter which Dakota had been concerned with. For money I would have to turn to people, who had invented it.

But the men who knew how to tinker with an ailing mortgage and keep it alive were no longer lending money to me or anyone else. Only government would help me lamb my sheep, and government's relation to a sheepman was the same relationship that existed between a textbook and life. Government lined up its facts in perpendicular columns and life didn't come that way.

I felt qualified to deal with the irregularities and contingencies of a lambing season, but in dealing with government I was a novice. The man who took my application for a loan was good-natured and openhanded, and he was also a novice. The first time he took hold of a ewe's head to open her mouth and see how old she was, I knew at once that he didn't know anything about sheep. A sheepman would have stood behind the ewe, pulled her lip down to expose her teeth, and would have learned her age without embarrassing the ewe. But government faced the ewe, pried her mouth open with both hands as though planning to crawl in headfirst and thoroughly aroused the ewe's suspicions. She shook free and government never learned how old she was.

"She's a young ewe," the man said. "How many have you, and how much money do you want?"

If I had known government well I would have asked for ten thousand dollars and left for Mexico on the next train. But I was a sheepman who had just lifted the mortgage from his sheep and didn't want to get any further into debt on them than was absolutely necessary. I borrowed enough money to hire lambing help and no more, believing that my shearing check would see me through the summer. I signed the paper, and though I had read the clause which stated that all products of the band of sheep became the property of the Regional until the debt had been discharged, I thought nothing of it at the time.

I lambed in May in a downpour of rain. Day after day the ranks of clouds swept over my shedless prairie lambing — chilling, killing and disowning lambs, shackling my every movement in mud. Dakota was throwing the whole book at me again. Dakota didn't know that there was a Dust Bowl. It had never used the word. Dakota didn't know that this was the Big Drought, it was just raining because it felt that way.

The drought-weakened grass slowly responded. The weeds came up first, and some of them were poisonous. The slowness of the grass compelled the sheep to eat weeds. In one morning I witnessed the sudden violent death of ten lambs.

Then the grass came, and the wheat leaped, and the vista from sky line to sky line was one of lush plenty. The hundred acres of grain was knee-high and a dark, rich green. The four hundred acres I hadn't been able to plant was hip-high in ragweed and sunflowers by mid-July.

About this time, when the prairie was promising fat lambs, haystacks, and fifty-bushel wheat, and only men were withholding money, I received a glowing letter from Scribner's which contained everything but money. "Your story attracted a great deal of attention among the editors," the letter said. "What are you doing? Have you ever tried writing a book?" Praise, but no money. Money, it appeared, would have to come from ranching after all.

I looked at the years '30, '31, and '32. Dakota seemed to be using a tom-tom beat — two bad years, followed by a thumper. It seemed to me that in a country as lavish as this country was when in an abundant mood, a man could keep his sheep alive on one good year in three if he had the brains to recognize the rhythm and act upon it.

I had the biggest crop in sight that I had ever seen upon this land. The grain would fill my granaries and I would have to heap it on the ground. The four hundred acres that I hadn't planted, if I could only cut it for hay, would yield four hundred tons of feed. But I lacked money, and I hadn't yet learned the ways of government.

When a wool buyer offered me thirty cents a pound on my wool clip I thought I'd sell it and take the money. I was ready to sign the contract, but when he learned that the sheep were mortgaged to the government corporation he said, "I can't buy your wool," and put the papers away.

"Why not?" I asked.

"The Farm Board thinks that farmers should support their co-operatives and that now is the time to start. You've got to pool this wool in a co-operative, no two ways about it."

"Hell!" I said, "the co-op only pays a third down, and that isn't enough to run me through the summer!"

"It's worse than that," the buyer warned me. "The money you get from the co-op has to go to the Regional."

"That doesn't make sense!" I complained.

"You're telling me!" he said. Then he related the experience of a sheepman in Oregon who, a few weeks before, had applied for additional money to lamb five thousand ewes. The Regional replied that his security didn't justify additional advances. He wrote back that if they wanted to save the five thousand ewes at all they'd better get some money on the line to hire a lambing crew. They again refused, and suggested that he could lamb the sheep himself without help by *lambing a limited number of ewes daily.*

"What did he do?" I asked.

141

"He fired the herders he had and let the sheep go to hell," he answered. "And they went there too, don't you think for a minute they didn't."

I couldn't do that, so I applied for additional funds.

My request was neither accepted nor refused. It simply dropped into a silence as profound as that which had followed the submission of my story. Meanwhile Dakota was yielding nothing to the unhurried coffee drinking of government clerks and the endless postponement of interoffice communication. While they pondered and ignored, the season marched ahead a day at a time.

The weeds got ripe and became worthless for hay. The grain got ripe and I had no money to buy twine or gasoline. A letter came from the Regional, a printed form which read: "If you still desire the sum applied for, fill out the enclosed blank and return to this office."

There was only one thing to do. I upended my safe-deposit box and gleaned all the odds and ends of common stocks. I took this pitiful dab and dumped it on a ruinous market, receiving enough money to buy gasoline and twine.

Thus, a bountiful harvest became an unhappy race with poverty. As I circled the hayfields on the Farmall, the sickle tumbled a dense swath, but I didn't gloat over it, I worried instead about the amount of fuel left in my barrels. As I circled the grainfields pulling a binder through a fifty-bushel-to-the-acre grain crop, and the binder fired bundles like a machine gun, I begrudged every yank upon that ball

a pendulum swinging back and forth between good years and bad, a bad year was coming up. But '27, '28, and '29 had been uniformly good. Perhaps '33 could be another '32, which had started dry.

There was no way of knowing. I could only farm cheaply as many acres as I could cover, and keep my band of sheep for a hedge against hail and drought.

I took the big tractor into the field with a disc and a drill behind the disc. I farmed two hundred and fifty acres for less than a dollar an acre, while a herder held the sheep in the south pasture.

The year rolled on and it was neither wholly good nor wholly bad. In due course of time I accepted a score that was almost — but not quite — like that of our first year on the ranch. Though the cracked earth stared at me through the grass that I had cut the year before, a better variety of wheat yielded ten bushels where our first wheat crop had yielded five, my oats returned twenty for one, and my mowers found a first cutting of alfalfa hay. Under the same conditions of rainfall that had blanked us before, I came through the year with my shirt intact.

In March, on the first anniversary of Roosevelt's inaugural address, an emissary of the New Deal appeared in my barn. The man was a neighbor of mine, and I didn't recognize him at first as an emissary of government. I thought he had come to borrow machinery, or perhaps to buy some

147

seed. But I soon learned that he was a Greek bearing gifts. He had come, he said, to offer me money for not raising hogs, for reducing my wheat acreage and for refraining from planting corn.

I had read the opinions of Henry Wallace, and before that had listened to the cursing of the Farm Board. They both proceeded on the theory that farmers were greedy men who had to be protected from themselves. I had no intention of being protected from myself.

I didn't think there was a surplus as long as there were people anywhere in the world who didn't have enough to eat. And how were these textbook politicians to outguess drought? They didn't even know how to look into a sheep's mouth. How were they to know which way the weather was going to jump next when the weather itself hadn't decided yet? How were they to know that Famine might not come next year, in a bad drought? A real Famine this time, with bins empty all over the United States and people hungry because there was no food? I thought I knew something about famine and surplus because I had seen and felt both. But I doubted that either Henry Wallace or Franklin Roosevelt knew the first thing about either. Certainly I was not going to let them protect me from myself.

Government was offering to pay me money for not raising hogs. I had never raised a hog in my life. But I was raising a variety of rustproof wheat that could only be marketed by shipping it in carloads to Minneapolis and I fully intended to plant with a carload in mind.

"I don't raise hogs," I said shortly, "and not much corn. What I do raise and plan to plant is strictly my own business."

"You don't have to raise hogs to get the money," he pointed out. "All you have to do is *agree* not to raise hogs, and to plant less corn and wheat."

"My wheat acreage is just the way I want it," I said. "It's going to stay the way I want it, and if Roosevelt don't like it he can go straight to hell."

"That ain't any way to look at it," said my neighbor. "The government is going to cut down the wheat acreage one way or another. If we don't do it when they ask us to, they'll crack down and make us do it."

"They're not going to 'crack down' on me!" I said angrily, "not as long as I've got shells for my 30-30. This is my land and I'll put a hole through the first guy that tries to tell me what to do."

"Well, don't get sore at me about it," he said. "I'm just making a little money on the side by taking these applications around. The way I've got it figured, it's our money they're putting out, and we might as well get our share of it while the getting is good. It'll be our taxes that will pay for it in the end. But if you don't want the dough, that's your business."

I was ashamed. "No hard feelings for you personally," I said, "but I don't want any part of this government money. I've had government money, all I ever want to see of it."

But Dakota was not interested in saving me from the

necessity of taking government money any more than it was interested in saving Henry Wallace the task of dealing with real Famine. That year the tom-tom missed a beat, and we had a thumper of a drought.

I had come to regard the arrival of green grass in the spring as an inalienable right, something that was as sure to come as Easter. A Swede neighbor of mine always pronounced the words "green grass" as though they were one word, thereby making it less a color and more an event, which of course it is.

It was an event which had an immediate effect upon sheep. Once they had tasted the tender green shoots, they lost appetite for either hay or sun-ripened grass on which they grazed contentedly enough during the winter. Once the first blades of green appeared, their grazing suddenly took on the aspects of an Easter egg hunt. They ran from blade to blade, poured along the draws, swarmed up the hills. Herding them through this brief period was a foot race, and it was one of the virtues of March lambing that the race occurred after the lambing operation, not simultaneously with it.

This neurotic quest was the prologue to Greengrass proper. Greengrass proper was the event that stopped this foot race in its tracks and left the spread quiet for long hours under the spring sun. It was an event in which the tall grasses got the idea first because they had more growth to accomplish in the allotted time; the small prairie flowers blossomed next, because they had less to lose if the weather proved them wrong. The short grasses, because they were careful and planned to live forever, never ventured far from the soil, and sent their first green through the dead stalks of last year's growth before planning and executing new conquest. Then, all at once, the yellow violets were up on the southern slopes, the buttercups took the blue shale breaks, lavender and white phlox was out like a rash of color on every barren ridge, yucca sent up its altar candles from the spiny heart of the old growth, the plum and thorn apple bushes in the thickets exploded into bloom, and Greengrass was an accomplished fact. Dakota never wore a broader, warmer smile than at this season of the year.

But Dakota did not smile in the spring of 1934. The sun had peered down unblinkingly through a warm, dry April, and as the days moved on, it came in closer to glare upon a hot, dry spring. As I planted wheat in mid-April, the hills still rolled toward the sky line wearing the old cloak of last year's grass. The sun saw nothing that it had not seen in January, and it peered still closer, searing the thin green shoots that had appeared in spots where small snowdrifts had stood.

The sheep soon ceased to run, for there was nothing to run for. Nor did they do well upon the old dead grass. To my troubled eyes the lambs seemed smaller than when they had left the lambing corrals in March.

In mid-May the water holes began to shrink, the wheat

lay exhausted after having achieved a four-inch growth. The corn hadn't sprouted. Then rain clouds appeared, and for a brief time it seemed that rain might happen. But only a thin pattering could be heard on the roof. For several days the clouds floated by, alternating sunlight with an occasional misty rain, long enough to fool the wheat and deceive some of the corn. Then the clouds went away again and left the betrayed plants to die.

The hope of a wild hay crop died in April, the alfalfa and wheat prospects followed in May, hope of a corn crop in June. During the misty spell the sheep had run briefly, finding some green grass. But the sun soon stared the grass out of countenance, and in temperatures of 105, looked down upon a countryside that still wore last year's castoff garments. The sheep pressed desperately and continuously upon the fence lines, hoping that somewhere, somehow, green grass could be found.

The sheepherders wore out and I replaced them one at a time. But Mike, the sheep dog, I couldn't replace. He was the only dog who really knew the job, my pups were too young, and green herders needed an experienced dog to teach them the ropes. They used Mike endlessly, to the very limit of his endurance. He grew lame, for cactus had increased under drought conditions and even the grass was little better to a dog's naked pads than a bed of splinters. Mike's feet became cracked, his coat dull, his eyes mattered and sore.

I sent two men out with the sheep. One was an old crackpot who had condescended to work for a time while he was waiting for the Townsend pension. The other was a young boy, marking time until he could get into a CCC camp. Between them and the dog, they preserved a precarious domination over the sheep.

Early in June the water holes gave up. Three weeks later the wells quit. I hauled water, working sixteen hours a day on hot days in an effort to keep the troughs full, but never could I really haul enough.

Meanwhile the panic was on. Cattlemen, who knew by now that there would be no haystacks for winter, and fearful of their dwindling water, began to ship to market in increasing numbers.

One day I was held up at a railroad crossing for twenty minutes while a stock train rolled through town from the north. From the slatted cars panting livestock peered out at me in a bewilderment equal to my own. They didn't know where they were going any more than I knew where I was going. As the cars clacked by over the switch near the crossing, my eyes kept track of the kind of stock that was moving:

. . . clack, clack, clack, clack, cattle, cattle, cattle, cattle, sheep, cattle, cattle sheep cattle, cattle, cattle. . . .

Not many sheep were going yet.

The sound of the train faded away in the direction of market, but the radio took up the tale of their arrival.

"Cattle receipts in Omaha today, thirty-five thousand, market slow. . . .

"Cattle receipts in Omaha today, forty-thousand, market inactive. . . .

"Cattle receipts in Omaha today, forty-five thousand, hold-over 40,000. . . ."

. . . cattle, cattle, cattle, cattle, cattle, CATTLE!

They couldn't go and they couldn't stay. Where now, brown cow?

There were two answers. Of the two, Dakota's answer was the simplest. "Lie down and die, brown cow, bogged to the belly in the stinking mud of a dead water hole." The other answer was government.

The rumors of a government program for buying cattle began to be heard almost at once, but even those who were pro-New Deal were apprehensive of government domination. Cracking down was very much on the lips of the Washington hierarchy. The news headlines were full of the fines and punishments meted out by government agencies which had no legal status, and yet could try offenders and punish them without jury trial.

When an actual cattle-buying program was announced the rattling of chains could be heard in it. Wallace was not ready to say how many cattle we should keep and how many we should sell. He didn't know yet how many cattle he wanted in the United States. So a form had been prepared for this contingency. In it the seller agreed to agree to any future agreement submitted by the Secretary of Agriculture.

An agreement to agree to something we had not yet seen,

154

looked like a cocked pistol. Up to that time we had been trained to honor our signatures. The signing of the agreements was slow.

But Dakota pushed. Our stock was leaning on the fences, it was trailing long miles to bad water, some of it was bogging, some of it was dying of thirst. My truck was running day and night, and barely keeping even with the job. I had thirty-five cattle that I was watering from city mains. They drank as much water as my entire band of sheep. I wanted to sell the cattle, but it was a hard pill for me to agree.

The buying started at the railroad loading pens, with one day a week set aside for the receiving of stock from my neighborhood. On that day the roads leading to town would be plumed at intervals of half a mile with clouds of dust from trailing cattle. The committeemen waited at the yards to receive and appraise them.

The committeemen were local cowmen recruited for the occasion from the ranks of the politically sound. But they were cowmen first of all, and no more pleased with the notion of accepting coercion from Washington than the rest of us were. As a consequence the agreement to reduce cattle numbers, which the secretary planned to submit later, was sabotaged in advance. There was a little square on the application blank in which the signer declared the number of cattle he had on hand. The committeeman suggested that each signer make a liberal allowance for the future.

A MAN FROM SOUTH DAKOTA

With my tongue in my cheek, I signed the agreement to agree, and in due course of time received a check which was double the amount the cattle would have brought at market.

The moral of this experience wasn't lost on me. Government, no matter how hairy-chested it might appear to be, had a blind side. I saw that the planning of the Planners was another of the hazards of agriculture that could be avoided by any private planner who had eyes. There was nothing in my rule book that prevented me from taking this sucker's money. And neither Dakota nor government had enough power to make a Democrat out of a Dakotan.

Chapter XI

THE GROUND THAT WAS UNDER ME

MY FIELDS were dry and dusty in March, and it seemed a forlorn hope to place any farming bets on the board for the 1935 season. But out of the wreckage of the 1934 drought I had harvested a field of Mindum Durum wheat. It wasn't enough to ship to market, and the mill wouldn't buy it, but there was enough to plant one hundred and fifty acres. In 1932 I had learned the penalty of not keeping the board covered with bets. So I also bought some oats and rounded out a full planting of small grain.

On the heels of this planting I squeezed in fifty acres of corn planting. By the time I finished this work, further planting would have been out of the question, because a four-inch rain was followed by a week of drizzle — and after a brief period of sunlight — by still another heavy rain. Once again two dry years were succeeded by a seambuster.

I saw the harvesting squeeze coming before it arrived. The barley, planted late, was going to ripen at the same time as the early wheat, and the oats gave every indication of doing the same thing. The wild hay came on early as well, and some of it was high enough to cut by the time we got through with the alfalfa.

A solution presented itself in the form of a chance to put the sheep in a summer herd in the Breaks twenty miles east of the ranch. Getting the sheep out of the way for the summer would not only save my grass and give the lambs fresh feed when they came home in the fall, but it would free a man whom I could use on the harvest.

The result was that I had two young men, both of them good mechanics, when the barley was ready to bind. But I had only one binder, and the grain, too heavy for its straw, was beginning to lodge and mat against the ground.

It was a hectic week. We bolted a bucket to the axle of the tractor and after sundown set a gasoline lantern in it, wrapped around its base with sacks to soften the shock from the tractor. We hung another from the rear of the binder, suspending it from a spring, and tying it solidly at the bottom so that it rode smoothly with its weight on the spring. With one man on the binder, one on the tractor, and one sleeping on a tarp near the field, we kept the binder in motion for ninety-six hours without stopping it for anything but grease and twine.

During my turns of sleep on the tarp, it was a comfortable sensation to have nothing between me and the stars but the soft night air, and to hear the patient motor cheating Time. Something was going on in the field that was not connected with dollars, or with employer-employee relationships. Three men were working together to beat

Dakota at its own game. If Dakota could work all night, so could we.

When the lambs came home from the summer range, every acre of hay had been put up on the same terms. The cornfields were clean of weeds, and though the corn had been planted late, it was a short early-maturing variety suitable for fattening lambs. Six weeks after the lambs went into it I corraled and shipped them. For the first time in nine years of sheep growing, lambs of mine topped a terminal market, bringing a dime a hundred more than any others sold that day.

My bets had all paid off, and I had a surplus of hay just in case Dakota decided to reverse itself again and achieve another dry year.

There had been a time when Distance had a meaning in Dakota, when thirty miles behind a team was a stiff day's travel, when news circulated by team or saddle horse and by those means only. Since grocery stores and coal-yards were far away, autumn saw a ranch well-stocked for a long siege, its larders filled, its fuel bins bulging.

But Distance had lost the old terror. The automobile had drawn its sting. Thirty miles an hour was now our rate of travel, or sixty if our mood was right. Town and coal and groceries were a matter of minutes, not of hours. Occasionally, automobiles were helpless when gumbo rolled up on the tires after a heavy rain. But drought and road machines had given us well-drained, hard-packed roads and they were seldom impassable for more than two or three days. So we ceased to worry about Distance.

When the blizzard hit in January of '36, we were accustomed to buying our groceries and coal and wood on the picayunish scale of honeymooning brides. We bought for the week, not for the months. And, when Dakota reminded us that its distances still packed a wallop, we had only one of the old weapons with which to defend ourselves, the telephone line.

The telephone wire looped across the miles which lay between our ranches. It arched its way down the more populous creek bottoms, it branched at any point to pick up a stray bachelor in the Breaks, and on the upland where ranches were more widely scattered, it staggered across the empty miles in long, zigzagging strides.

The instruments themselves dated from the horse-and-buggy days. The telephone was screwed firmly to the wall at a Spartan height, and at the base of the oaken box there was a jutting shelf on which short people could chin themselves to reach the mouthpiece and talk. On the side of the box was the "rubbering switch," a device which kept our voices off the line while we listened to things which were none of our affair. It hadn't however been devised as an incentive to eavesdropping, but to spare our batteries the task of broadcasting over the line our heavy breathing and the ticking of our clocks. On the other side of the box was the crank which summoned a quorum to the "rubbering switch."

THE GROUND THAT WAS UNDER ME

It wasn't a perfect system of communication. Too many horses had scratched themselves on its poles, too many frost storms had sagged its wires, too many subscribers — pinched by Depression — hadn't paid their bills. But it still got Distance, it was still an echoing tunnel in which doors opened and closed, and eyes peered from behind window curtains. It was our dumb-waiter, our messenger boy, and our life line.

On Mondays one heard every washing between the mountains and the river being hung out a second time on the telephone wire. On Tuesdays, Wednesdays and Thursdays one could hear tidings of the neighborhood's chronic invalids and their constant struggle with such things as kidneys and high blood pressure. On Fridays one could hear the high-school students calling from town the reasons why they couldn't come home to work over the week end; and on Saturday nights bachelors canvassed the schoolteacher situation in self-conscious mumbles. Every day in the week, promptly at nine A.M., there was a weather report.

One morning in January of 1936 the operator said: "Here is the weather report. Snow and much colder. High, shifting winds. Protect livestock."

One wouldn't have guessed it. The sky was clear, the air was warm, the ground was dry and free from snow. But I sent the hired man out for a load of hay and hiked for town with the car to get food and tobacco.

That night the snow came in on a high wind. It roared

161

past our windows in a steady sweep, it buffeted the house and buildings until midnight. Then the wind stopped and the mercury dived for the bulb. It was thirty below.

Once again Dakota didn't know when to stop. We had seen storms like this last three or four days, but we have never seen one last six weeks, and we had never heard of fifty-two below.

Mornings, when the sun came up, the earth might be as still as death, and from sky line to sky line there would be nothing to see but white. The black of the pines would be masked in ice; the Butte which usually thrust some shoulder through the heaviest snow would be a spike of chrome steel. None of it would bear looking at — it had a glitter that was a hot sheen on one's eyeballs.

Then the wind would come up, slowly gathering might. A white haze would march across the glistening land, whispering crisply on the icy crust. Then plumes would grow to clouds, the light of the sun would disappear, the air would be full of flying snow, and the cold would be doubled by the penetration of the wind.

A wind from the north on one day might be followed by a wind from the south on the next. The snow was never still for long, it was constantly filling in old hollows, cresting in new waves.

An automobile had no chance. The snow was too hard for a car to rush through a drift on momentum, but not hard enough to bear its weight. There was little open ground through which a car might pick a path. Traveling anywhere meant shoveling foot by foot, and when the shoveling was done, say an hour of it for half a mile, a wind could scoop it all shut in five minutes. Nor did a man have a chance of walking any distance in that cold, for at any moment a wind might come up, catch him far from shelter, and leave him there a chunk of ice like the rest of it.

We did our chores at a high run, handling forks and scoops whose handles seared the hands like hot coals. At short intervals we galloped for the house to thaw out frozen members. We did our work in installments, interrupted by respites in which we cherished our red-hot stoves.

Every night our radios blared into our ears harrowing accounts of our own sufferings. In tones filled with dire foreboding, skilled newscasters upended their *Rogets'* into our laps. "King Winter holds Midwest in icy grasp as thermometer plummets to new lows," they said. "Storms rage on midwest prairies bringing suffering and starvation in their wake," they said.

We didn't recognize ourselves. We thought that the boys north of the River must be catching hell, and they wondered why — if we were that hungry — we didn't knock over a cow.

The voices one heard over the telephone didn't seem to be in any acute pain. They were casual, rather than dire, and just a little inclined to gloat over the intensity of the whole thing. Most of our sufferings appeared to be minor.

"Say, Bill," I heard a voice say, "have you got any tobacco over there? I've been smoking some stuff my wife uses to keep moths out of the carpets. It don't burn, it explodes."

On "cross talk," a phenomenon common on windy days when the wires of the entire system would become crossed, and would link us all together in one big unhappy family, a faint conversation could be heard: ". . . Seven tons of coal at the schoolhouse. Whyn't you drive down with the spring wagon and get a load?"

Often someone would get the urge to mount a saddle horse and sprint for town. At such times the hero would announce his intention and do errand work for those who couldn't go. I went in twice and came back heavily laden, mostly with tobacco and coffee and matches, commodities on which enforced leisure made a heavy drain.

Fortunately my barn loft was full of hay. When the coal and wood gave out we were worried but not particularly fearful, for there were enough fence posts in sight to last us to July.

The newscasters meanwhile were having a hard time. Nothing much had happened but cold, and cold as a column-one story had gone far past that magic Ninth Day. The newscasters' vocabularies were down to skin and bone. Meanwhile the telephone line unearthed a Nine Day Wonder that was column-one news.

"Hello, Central," a woman's voice said one morning, "get me the airport."

The wire, which had been carrying four or five conversations on as many lines, was suddenly stilled.

THE GROUND THAT WAS UNDER ME

The phone buzzed and a receiver clattered off the hook. A girl's voice said, "Airport."

"Why-uh," our woman's voice came over the wire, at a loss as to how to state her problem. "I wonder if I could get a plane to come out twenty-eight miles to get a sick man. And I'd like to know how much it would cost."

The reply was not what we had expected.

"Oh we couldn't possibly get a plane out today," the girl replied. "We're snowed in up here. None of our pilots are around."

"Could you find one of the pilots so I could talk to him?" our woman persisted. "It's my husband and he's awful sick. I'm afraid it's appendicitis."

The office girl gave our woman a name and a number.

"I'll ring that number for you," our Central said.

The phone buzzed several times. Then it was answered by another woman.

Our woman gave the pilot's name and asked to talk to him.

"Call later," was the reply. "He isn't up yet."

We looked at our clocks. Ten o'clock in the morning! Holy smoke!

I waited for the voice of the birdman, the hero in helmet and goggles, I waited for: AVIATOR WINGS WAY OVER DRIFTS TO SAVE APPENDICITIS VICTIM FROM DEATH.

But all I heard was a voice with fur on its tongue saying, "Whatcha want?"

Our woman stated her case. There was a long pause.

"I can't get a plane off the ground," he said finally. "The airport is snowed in and I couldn't land out there anyway. Call the airport and see if you can't get hold of the government inspector. He's supposed to come in this morning and he's got skis on his plane." He hung up.

Central called the airport. But the government inspector wasn't there. He had come in early and left for Cheyenne.

Our woman was persistent. She called the pilot again.

She had him on a spot. She wanted a hero and he didn't feel like being one. Finally he said, "Is there any place to land out there?"

"There's a big smooth field right in front of the house," our woman replied. "There's some snow on it, but I'll shovel it off if you'll tell me how big a place you need to land."

A voice interrupted without apology. "My man will come over and help."

The aviator said he'd see if he couldn't get the county blade to clear a lane on the airport. But fifteen minutes later the air was filled with flying snow. . . .

As usual Dakota didn't know when to stop. Three days later the man was still out there, still sick, still needing desperately to get to town. The pilots didn't have skis on their planes. They couldn't get the airport cleared. Then they were expecting skis on the train. But the train couldn't get in. . . .

166

THE GROUND THAT WAS UNDER ME

At this point some bungling idiot repaired the crossed wires and we lost our story. A little while later we lost Central.

Five days after the woman had first called the airport I picked up the receiver and learned that the situation was continuing but that it seemed to be approaching some sort of climax.

". . . Truck with some hay in it. My man is out shoveling our stretch and I see somebody coming across from Johnson's with a team and some men in a wagon. . . ."

I waited.

. . . They're coming by now. I guess they ought to make it. The road is clear now as far as the crick, and I can see a team standing up there on the Divide. . . ."

They got him to town. Twenty-eight miles.

He died a week later of cancer. But he died in a hospital, under a doctor's care.

The storm went on without him. It went down to fifty-two below. It crept back to twenty-five below. There was more wind, more snow. Then one day a brown haze appeared on the mountains to the west. A chinook. Slowly it poured down off the mountains and spread over the Butte. Fantastically the Butte climbed to towering heights, in a mirage. It was just being built . . . the scaffolding was all that held the top of it up . . . you could see through it . . . they hadn't put the siding on yet. . . . Then the water was dripping off our eaves and the Butte was itself again.

With a whoop, the whole neighborhood came out of the trenches. Road information shuttled back and forth along the telephone line.

"You better not take the road past our place. There's a big drift at the foot of the hill." . . . "You better go in the north gate . . . you can get through that way. . . ."

By noon a maze of slush filled ruts pointed toward town. They wound around through pastures, dodging drifts searching for routes across ditches. They doubled back upon themselves and explored brand-new country never visited by automobiles before. My speedometer registered sixteen miles for an eight-mile trip.

I didn't stay in town long. I loaded the car with groceries, collected the hired man from his pool hall, and started for home. I didn't trust the weather because I had never seen a chinook that wasn't followed by a high north wind.

The storm was upon us when we topped the last hill above the ranch. It swirled around the car as we unloaded the supplies.

Twenty-five below and fresh snow.

Perhaps the radio newscasters had some new words for it. I didn't listen, for the telephone line was again carrying the better story. Almost every family had someone at home and someone out in the storm. The line was never still, and from wall to wall, from door to door, that echoing tunnel was filled with voices.

"Hello Mabel, have you seen anything of Dave coming by?"

"Hello, Haggerty's, well say, I was wondering if you've seen the folks?"

"Hello, Helen, Bill just got home. He said Dave hadn't started yet. Said he saw him on the street in front of the creamery."

"Why, they're out here now, Joe. They're stuck in the drift below the barn. My man's gone out to tell them to stay here tonight."

"Is that you *Dave*? Oh, Dave, thank the Lord. No, don't you do it. I'll milk the cows, you stay right where you are."

One by one the telephone accounted for its people. Some called from town, some turned up in warm houses, and some called from the homes of neighbors they hadn't spoken to in years.

Supper put no end to the talk, the sounds of mastication were audible over the wire. And the wire, warm and cozy with the sound of human voices, hummed in the wind across the terrible miles.

This, I thought, *is a stiff-necked people!*

Dakota had muffed it again. What it would try next lay over the sky line in Next Year.

Chapter XII

THE RAIN OF MY LAND

THE HEAVY winter feeding, made necessary by the endless storm and cold, had cut into the surplus of hay which the bountiful summer of 1935 had produced. The sharp expansion in my band had at the same time made itself felt. With the thermometer at thirty-five below, the sheep, held up in the corrals, and cut off from grass, had consumed hay at the rate of three or four stacks a week.

My margin of safety was reduced, but not alarmingly so. The snow would start the first cutting of alfalfa whether more rain fell or not, and it would make good early grass. Furthermore, the sheep were contracted to go to the summer herd again which would also reduce the burden on my grass. I planted more corn and planned to fatten more lambs.

But Dakota had other intentions for the snow. The last blizzard piled all of it in steep banks on the south side of the hills. The rest of the soil was bare. When a chinook moved down from the hills and turned the drifts to water, the water poured down the draws in a brief flood, then all the ground was bare.

In time a whiskering of green appeared on the narrow spots where the drifts had stood, but elsewhere the grass showed no signs of life. The corn I planted did not come up. I had planted it carefully with a lister, a tool which deposited the kernel in a moisture-conserving ditch. These ditches followed the contours of the land, so that torrential rains would not pour down them and wash the corn away.

But no rain fell.

I sheared the sheep and sent them down the trail to the summer range, and still no rain fell.

The summer grazing lease upon which I was counting so heavily was a large area known as the Alkali Breaks. Beginning at the edge of a high, level plateau, its acres dropped, through a long tangle of rough draws and blue shale cutbanks, toward the Belle Fourche River several miles distant. It was an area so tip-tilted that it had never known the plow. There was no water in all this wilderness of grassland except for a big stock dam in the center of the lease. The snowdrifts had filled it. Even the antelope and coyotes were watering there. Beyond the line of our lease, cattle trudged down the dusty trails to water in the Belle Fourche.

The range looked green when we dropped into it from the south, but this was an illusion, as we soon found out. For here too we were seeing thinly-grassed southern slopes where drifts had stood. The flats and the northern slopes wore nothing but 1935 grass. It was impossible to calculate the staying power of those green areas. Hoping against hope that there was more grass than I thought there was, I turned my back on this perplexity and resumed the ones I faced at home.

When I returned again to the Breaks a few days later, the herder said, "We've got to get out of here. There ain't any grass. I can't hold them in the daytime and they won't stay on the bedgrounds at night. Last night I caught them half a mile from the wagon. They were hungry and hunting for grass. We got to find some more room."

I heard a rumor that there was a lease to be had up in the mountains. I drove a hundred miles to find that it wasn't true. I heard another rumor that there was grass to be had forty miles east of the Breaks. I drove in that direction, stopping to ask the way of a group of farmers who were working on a WPA project along the road. I continued on my way for another thirty miles and inquired again for the man who had advertised for sheep to graze.

"Oh hell," my informant answered, "that was a long time ago. His grass blew up and he sold the sheep he had. He's working up there along the road somewhere on WPA."

I talked to him on the way back, and while I was thus engaged, another man came up and offered to sell me eleven hundred acres of grass. The figure he named should have bought the land as well, but I had to have room and I went to look at his grass.

There was deep shade along the creek, and though the creek wasn't running, there were water holes at frequent intervals along its dry bed. The 1935 growth hadn't been grazed off the year before, and along the creek bottom there was a green stand. I wrote the man the check that clinched the deal and went back to the Breaks to move camp.

A week later when I came out to the new lease I asked the herder how he was getting along.

"I ain't getting along at all," he said. "There isn't nothing left now but last year's grass. They're eating it, but we've got too many sheep to hold on this much land. And the crick is boggy. I can only water at the upper end. I had to pull out forty head the first day — stuck in that blue mud. If you think it's any cinch holding twenty-eight hundred head on eleven hundred acres, you're crazy in the head."

"Can you do it with another man to help you?" I asked.

"Maybe," he said, "and I need a fresh horse. While you're at it you'd better bring me a bottle of vinegar. The water bags don't seem to cool the water down, even at night. I can drink hot water if it's a little sour. . . ."

I hired an extra man, bought some more water bags made of linen, and attempted to bring him a quart of ice cream.

He drank the ice cream and said, "You'd better bring me another dog. Sally is wore out."

I went home posthaste to get Mike, planning to bring him down the next day.

Something intervened at home and it was two days later when I approached the lease with Mike in the seat beside me. As I crossed the creek I came upon a water hole in our lease that was literally a shambles. It was filled from rim to rim with dead sheep. I hopped out of the car and dug around in the bodies. To my great relief the brand was strange to me.

"God Almighty!" I said to the herder. "What happened down there?"

"Happened yesterday while I was up here on the flat," he replied. "I saw these fellows coming from the north, and knew there was something wrong because they weren't making any time. They were yelling and swinging their coats, but the sheep didn't pay them any mind. Then a guy hopped into a car and came over to me. He wanted to buy Sally. I asked him what was the matter with his dogs. He said they'd picked up some poison bait two days before. His sheep had already been off water two days and he had to have a dog. He offered me fifty bucks for Sally. I couldn't sell her because what the hell would *I* do without a dog? I asked him where he was going with the sheep and he said he didn't know for sure but he thought he could find some grass on the Reservation. I told him he'd better miss the bogs and water at the river. He said he aimed to, and how about loaning my dog until he got past the bogs.

"I wouldn't do it because a guy that needed a dog as bad as he did wouldn't bring her back. So they went on batting their sheep along the road. At the top of the hill the leaders all of a sudden smelled water and piled down over the hill into the bog.

"From here it looked to me like the sheep was piled in there ten deep. I seen those fellows trying to work around the edges to fight the rest back, but they kept a-piling in and a-piling in and finally these fellows just gave up and laid down on the ground under the trees. When I rode down there last night the guy said he'd lost two hundred head."

After what he had seen, the herder was more than glad to have Mike.

A week later when I came back to Elm Creek with supplies for the camp, a line storm was coming down across the Gumbo from the northwest. The sheep were spread along the creek banks and there was peril in the situation, for Elm Creek drains about forty miles of hardpan flats that shed water like a tin roof, and has a reputation for quick flash floods. The herder and I talked it over, and as the first drops of rain fell, decided it was time to get off the bottomland.

While the herder dogged the sheep together and got them to higher ground, I climbed in the car and crossed the creek to get a slicker at the wagon. Before I reached the wagon, the rain began to come down in solid sheets. It sluiced across my windshield like water from a fire hydrant. I couldn't see the radiator cap, let alone the road. Then, quite suddenly, the rain turned to hail. A barrage of hailstones as large as eggs began to strike the car and bound away. They struck the ground with the impact of well-hit baseballs, bounding and splashing and filling the air with fountains of muddy water. This lasted for about twenty minutes.

A MAN FROM SOUTH DAKOTA

The herder I knew had taken a beating, so I got out of the car and waded across the rising stream to see how he was faring. To my dismay I saw sheep standing under the trees along the creek bank. They had gotten away from the herder to seek shelter there. The herder was also hunched under a tree.

Water was already flowing onto the flood plain from the surrounding hills, but this wasn't a drop in the bucket when compared to what might be coming from those hardpan flats. We lost no time in gathering up the scattered bunches of sheep and in urging them across the bottom toward high land.

But the sheep were bewildered and sullen from the beating they had taken, and were in no hurry to go anywhere. They milled soddenly. We attacked them with flailing slickers, while the dogs, taking their cue from the anger and fear in our voices, lashed savagely at their heels and flanks. The band began to move.

As the water on the flood plain grew perceptibly deeper, inch by inch we rolled that milling wheel across the flat. Seldom did our eyes leave the bend in the creek where the water from the Gumbo would appear. At last we neared the bank, only to discover that we were stopped — an old channel of the creek bed lay across our path. It was full of water and too deep for sheep to cross.

Desperately we searched upstream and down for shoaling water that might indicate a crossing. At last we found a spot where the water was less than a foot deep. We dogged the sheep upstream to this point, but they again refused to cross. They stood there, maddeningly, while time raced by. We had to do something *now*. Then a familiar maneuver came to mind — one we used at bridge-heads when the sheep balked. We had no bridge railing to work against but I had Mike.

"Mike!" I said. "Go around them on *that* side!"

Obedient to the waving of my left hand, he worked around the left side of the band until he reached the crossing. I waved him down.

"Stay there!" I commanded.

"Now, let's mill 'em," I called to the herder.

Recognizing my plan, he put his dog to work, driving the outer edges of the band in a circle that turned to the right. It was a big wheel that scraped against Mike on the far side.

Mike's head went down, he was fighting them back. Still the wheel turned. Held by Mike in front and pushed by Sally from behind, there was only one place for the sheep to go — out into the stream. At last a leader splashed across, and the rest followed.

Not two minutes after the sheep had crossed to safety we heard the water coming. We also saw it and smelled it at the same time, for the wall of water had gouged out miles of stagnant bogholes and bore the stench on its crest. The crest marched down across the flooded plain and under our eyes the ground where we had stood became a living, roaring mass of water, high and tumbling in the middle, low and

177

swirling on the sides. It would have been an added humiliation to have drowned in such a stinking mess.

I petted Mike and thanked him as I would have thanked a man. He was pleased but not unduly impressed. He looked past me at the sheep and his eyes asked me a question. I followed his gaze, and saw that the sheep were running. Only the drag end was in sight.

The sheep ran all the rest of the afternoon, we couldn't hold them anywhere. The next morning we discovered why — there wasn't any grass. The brittle stalks had been pounded to bits by the hail and the water had washed them away. The hills of virgin prairie sod were as barren and black as freshly harrowed fields, but not as smooth. They were gullied and rough, gouged deeply by running water. The next day we trailed back to our old lease in the Alkali Breaks where, fortunately, it hadn't rained.

The rain of my land I saw could be a most confusing thing. Withheld for months, it would come, nine inches of it, in twenty minutes. The two hundred sheep that Drought had slain with thirst, the rains of Drought washed away. Twenty-four hours later the creek was again dry, and dust was blowing off the scalded acres which had never known the plow, while on the flat above the breaks, where the plow had been for four generations, Russian thistles were coming to life in orderly squares of green.

Chapter XIII

AS THE BLIND GROPE

THE same soil which had invited the buffalo to dwell upon it had invited us to gamble. The same soil which had stamped out the buffalo was now squeezing us out of the game. The shiftless left first. The careless men who had gone fishing and left hay to rot in the windrow, lost their grip upon their land and went to other lands in search of a softer sun. The renters with large families departed to seek sanctuary on WPA, for Dakota did not suffer the small children to come unto it. A few married couples who had invested too heavily in furniture and comfort surrendered their land and sought occupations less accursed.

The bachelors seemed to be better gamblers. Their lives were leaner, their purpose less divided, their austerity concentrated their thoughts and their love upon their land, and their land granted them survival.

It was fortunate for single men that they possessed this capacity, for the New Deal agencies assumed that bachelors could look out for themselves. Single men were not welcome on WPA, and because they had no hungry wives

179

and children to embellish their application blanks, they seldom obtained subsistence checks, or consideration of any kind.

I was a bachelor. Though I didn't live in a bachelor home, I was the arbiter of its purse strings, and its chief provider. Had I been willing to ask for a subsistence check, my aunt and uncle would have filled the appropriate lines in the appropriate blanks. But none of us were willing. Neither Dakota nor government had changed our political convictions. It was a bitter pill to take anything from a regime we hated so much.

Yet I was in a bad way financially. The wrinkled apple, the round ball whirling through space, had been ignoring my needs too long. I needed money, and only government had money.

But government, it developed, had a kind of money that I could take with a clear conscience — I could play the Secretary of Agriculture for a sucker again.

Undismayed by the current mood of the Great Plains, the Secretary was pursuing his original intention of curtailing Surplus, and of putting an end to drought in the same stroke — by planting shelter belts and returning farmed acres to alfalfa. For this he was willing to pay me money.

Early in the summer of '36, when I was trailing to Elm Creek, word went around that the Secretary would pay seven dollars an acre for land returned to alfalfa. The land must be plowed and seeded and the seed bills kept for proof of the seeding. The land would then be measured and payment would eventually be forthcoming.

But as the summer progressed, and Dakota soil was too dry to accept the point of a plow, let alone provide moisture to sprout the expensive seed, the Secretary yielded to the mood of the weather, and word went around that this handsome sum could be earned simply by a token discing of the land in question. Plowing and seeding could be omitted.

In mid-July I rattled and banged my disc over a suitable acreage. I never felt sillier in my life. The ground was so hard that the disc floated on its surface — a single team could have pulled it because it wasn't cutting any soil. But here I was with fifteen horsepower tracing aimless circles on farmland in midsummer and it was with the greatest difficulty that I could imagine anyone paying seven dollars an acre for these dim scratches on Dakota soil. I wished mightily for a ten-cent rain shower, so that I could leave some mark that might earn that money. But Dakota didn't give a damn whether I earned any money or not.

In the fall a committeeman came to appraise the extent of my "soil conserving" virtue. I led him to the fields which I had disced, and between us we managed to find some of the scratches that I had made earlier in the summer. He stared unhappily at them. Then his eye sought out the sprawling patch of black where I had contoured my corn with a lister. The seed hadn't sprouted, the weeds hadn't grown, and the deep ditches still lay there, crossways of the slope. It looked like soil conserving to the committeeman.

"Let's look at that," he said. "I ain't got the heart to write this down as summer fallow."

We examined the cornfield, where the listed rows waited patiently for a rain to sprout the corn.

"Hell," he said, "that's the best piece of summer fallow I ever saw. How many acres of that have you got?"

I told him, and without further questioning he wrote the figure down.

"When do I get the dough?" I asked.

He shrugged.

"If the New Deal doesn't get tossed out on its ear," he said, "you may get it about planting time next year. But if Landon is elected they'll probably forget the whole thing. Personally I think you'll get it."

Not long afterward, I met another pre-election argument. I had gone to the theatre to forget my troubles. But before I could lose myself in the picture I had paid to see, I was forced to sit through one I hadn't paid to see. It was a picture that had been made, without my consent, with my money. It was called *The Plow That Broke the Plains*. I was its villain.

The picture opened with a map of the United States which showed my state in funereal black, a cancer at the heart of a prosperous nation, a part of the "Dust Bowl." As the picture unfolded a plausible voice repeated endlessly; "In a land of few rivers, no trees, and not enough rainfall. . . ." The first scenes showed a bunch of cattle grazing in lush grass. This, the picture said, was the prairies' God-given function. Then a man plowed afoot with a horse plow. He was followed by tractors with gang plows, then by a host of small tractors, plowing night and day. This was followed by Surplus, closed banks, financial disaster. Then came the swirling dust storm. As the dust clouds rolled, the pitiful plowmen, now refugees from the consequences of their plowing sins, departed for elsewhere in broken-down cars, leaving a gaping hole at the heart of the United States, a hole that only the New Deal could heal. The End.

I was too angry to remain to see the feature picture I had paid to see. I was appalled at this insidious lie which was so plausibly told. It would have been as true to say that a ship had roused an ocean storm as to say the plow broke these plains. I was furious that my money had been used to call my plow a villain.

The impact of this political power in its tremendous aggregate dismayed me. From the hills where I herded sheep there was little that was cheerful to be seen any-where. Dust swirled from plowed fields and unplowed grazing land alike. In a high wind it had the impact of bird shot, pelting one's skin to the point of pain, sifting into clothing, leaving grit on one's teeth. Now and then a frost-blackened Russian thistle would bumble swiftly down wind with the uneven pace of a hobbling cripple, to be trapped at last by a fence, where it waited for dust to bury it.

Within sight of my job, a WPA dam was in process of erection. A full two hours after I went to work, the ranchers employed on the project went to work. A little after ten o'clock in the morning a dust cloud would grow over the dam site as they slowly plied their teams back and forth, scraping dirt onto the dam. At noon the dust cloud settled and did not rise again for at least two hours. Then it resumed, only to cease for the day at four o'clock. A full day's pay for four hours' work.

The rest of us in the neighborhood worked far longer hours. Were we fools? Would it be better to sell out and cling to the apron strings of government? I couldn't see it that way.

But as I paced the hills ahead of my rambling band I was of two minds about the alternatives. The sheep were not an inspiring sight. The lambs were small and potbellied, more than a hundred ewes were missing, casualties of flood, trailing, and not enough water to drink. But I had seen these things before, and rain had come back. Was it not a time to keep on boring ahead, expanding at depression prices into a still bigger operation?

The summer had by some strange quirk renewed my optimism and vigor. In the face of adversity I had been far less discouraged than in the presence of embarrassing plenty. At the peak of my ranching prosperity in 1929 I had felt as old and discouraged as King Solomon in his temple, but now, resting on the very bottom from the standpoint of material success, I felt only an urge to climb, to choose any path that led upward. WPA, Social Security, financial safety did not lead upward — they leveled off and circled endlessly for no gain. Only risk, financial danger, and an intelligent gambling on the future offered me any escape from the futility that I instinctively hated.

The summer on the trail had awakened in me an ambition to get into sheep on a bigger scale. There was a glamour about the larger type of range operation that appealed to me. In the course of my travels I had come upon an opportunity to buy a large summer range. Two thousand acres of deeded river-bottom land was the key to ten thousand acres of rough grazing land, because all the water in this area was controlled by the deeded land. This range, barren now, would make a good spread when the rains returned. I could buy it now for fourteen hundred dollars — if I had fourteen hundred dollars. . . .

The contemplation of the ways in which I might acquire this sum was a welcome escape from the uninterrupted contemplation of my own scuffed boot toes. The patterns of escape in my neighborhood were not too numerous that fall. The heat of election had been a temporary respite. In it we had been able to submerge our petty worries in a big worry. But once it was over and the field of political contention was quiet, our private afflictions asserted themselves and it was necessary to escape in some way if only to preserve sanity.

Escape. One hears the word used as though it were somehow illicit and obscene, like smoking opium, or taking to drink. But one who seeks to escape is actually a hunter of safety, and there was nothing phony about our need for it. Our movie theatres, our magazines, our radios were the bombproof dugouts into which we withdrew from time to time to collect our scattered wits and heal our frazzled nerves.

Those with an appetite for western stories devoured pulp magazines by the armload. Some made a cult of the funny-men on the radio, looking to them nightly for relief from despair. Some bought soap wrappers and tried to win twenty thousand dollars. Some, more literal-minded than the rest, sold out and actually took to their heels.

None of these routes was wholly satisfactory to me. I couldn't lose myself in fiction, the pap was too thin. The funnymen on the radio were too brief. The comedians I saw in the movies could give me surcease for no longer space of time than the screen was bright with their antics. I had no wish to sell my land because I didn't believe that it was doomed or that the plow had cursed it. Most of all, I still thought it was theoretically possible for me to make a million dollars. I would however settle for fourteen hundred dollars. . . .

Day after day as I herded the sheep, I read books. By accident, or subconscious intention, I read biographies. I was interested in the lives of men who had reached the high hills. By this route I came upon the life of a man which I thought might make a movie, and fourteen hundred dollars. . . .

AS THE BLIND GROPE

The sheepherding role was one which rendered the actor peculiarly vulnerable to delusions of grandeur. Shepherds watching their flocks by night had heard angels sing. Moses, herding sheep on the Mount of Horeb, had seen a burning bush, and had come boiling down off that mountain one day to write a book that was still a Best Seller.

But I couldn't write while I was pursuing that rambling band — Dakota wouldn't let me. Nor could I write at night. Fatigue knocked me over by nine o'clock in the evening, and the blackest coffee was powerless to keep me awake. Dakota, from the day of Ezra Kind, had no sympathy for authors.

But the fact remained that I had seen a burning bush and that I wanted fourteen hundred dollars. I came boiling down off my hill one day determined to get away from Dakota long enough to write what I had in mind.

Borrowing to the hilt on my life insurance, I rented a room near the campus of my alma mater and wrote until my money was gone.

I didn't earn the fourteen hundred dollars. All I got out of it was a winter's practice in writing.

About the time my money ran out a letter came from Aunt Ida. "It looks awfully black here," she said. "Dust storms every day. Perhaps it would be wise for you to find some kind of a job back there. . . ."

What kind of a job?

The only thing that I knew well was a band of sheep. The only land that I wanted to live on, green or black, was

Dakota land. I dumped my winter's writing in an agent's lap and boarded the train for home.

Ten years before, driving a new Model T pickup, I had left that college town, on my way home to sell a ranch and write a book about my experiences as a South Dakota rancher. Now, ten years later, my heart was still fond for South Dakota and I wanted to defend it in prose. But what possible ending could I find for South Dakota when so much of its future hung so precariously in the balance? I had nothing whatsoever to express in its behalf except my own continued faith in it.

Chapter XIV

THE ENEMY WITHIN MY LAND

THE LAND I saw from the train window on my way home was a different land from that I had seen ten years before when I had passed this way to matriculate in the sheep business. Many things had moved, many things had changed. The winds had lashed Dakota's surf into dense clouds of black dust and had sent them crashing down upon the lives of the men whose towns rode the prairie hills.

The barns and silos lacked paint, the fences were drowned in soil, gray sandy drifts of it encroached upon the roads; the fields of Russian thistle, charred by the frosts of winter, still scarred the earth in squares of funereal black. Everywhere along the way I saw gangs of men working beside the red, white and blue signs of WPA. They were building roads which hauled no produce, heaping dams that held no water, they were working for wages that offered them only survival.

It wasn't necessary that I peer into dusty library stacks to know who these men were and by what routes they had come into this captivity. I could see their time battered automobiles parked beside the dust heaps on which they

189

worked, and know just why a cracked windshield had not been replaced and why a sedan door was tied shut with a rope. A *Saturday Evening Post* reporter could come blandly into their midst and report with a shrug, ". . . there has never been much grace to life on these prairies, and there are no nuances to be lost now in a general descent of poverty upon the land." But I knew those nuances and that they could be lost when faith in Next Year died.

In many of these men that faith was dead. The gossip that the plow had brought on this catastrophe was the thing that had killed it. Lacking this faith made these men guilty, made them the victims of their own folly. It warned them never to plow again. It denied them the right to believe in next year.

It was necessary to have peered through library stacks to know that they were not guilty, that this force which had struck them down had struck these very acres before. These drifts of dust were no more and no less hostile to human hope than the Great Ice Sheet, which had once locked the Great Plains in a frigid silence; and certainly they were not to be blamed upon human hands. Dust clouds had poured from these plains ten thousand years before the Sioux crossed from Asia, and would pour again. The force was bigger than human kind, its calendar moved on a different scale from that of human history.

I had learned these things in a geology classroom when the raging fire of scientific doubt had first blazed across my mind. I had known them ten years ago when my car crawled across the face of these plains. Then I had been willing to surrender the ultimate human hope to a black geological death. But after ten years I had come to love this sweep of land, and this race of gambling men. I was no longer content to accept a futile ending. For if any year were to have a value, there must be an infinite number of next years. Dakota was not the kind of soil which would permit a man to retire behind an Epicurean philosophy, or permit him to console himself that the catastrophe was remote. For, in Dakota, geology was never remote, it lurked no further away than tomorrow's sky line, and a man had to believe that he could somehow outwit this blind hostility or he couldn't stay on Dakota land.

None of the books which I had sought out during that decade had contented me as a resident of Dakota land. No serious authorship which had dared to base its premise on scientific doubt had peered into the lair of the future and returned with its hope unseared. The current books, Galsworthy, Struthers Burt, Dreiser, Bromfield, had all implied the ultimate futility of human effort. Struthers Burt had summed it up in a toast, "Here's to the human race, dumb and gallant fools!"

Nor had I found anything more cheerful in the books that had come to be called "Classics." In *Moby Dick*, Herman Melville personified this same evil force which surged beneath the motionless waves of my prairie ocean. To him it was the Great White Whale. The whale who maimed Captain Ahab and sank the *Pequod* with all hands on board was white because Melville believed that the Ice Sheet would come again and that human life would not survive it.

For years every author that I met in the pages of a book, aside from those who were content to prove endlessly that the course-of-true-love-does-not-run-smoothly believed that the human race was bucking a crooked game. Yet here I was, a defeated gambler, creeping home with less than five dollars in his pocket, stubbornly insistent that the game could be beaten. I was very much alone.

Once again I awoke to the fact that next year had become this year and that it was time to plant. As I planted I found that I was once more in the position of having to curse rain. Frequent showers hindered my planting and made the fields for days on end swampy bogs.

But as the season developed it became apparent that the great enemy still lurked beneath my acres, and that his number was legion.

During the winter, fourteen thousand of his eggs lay dormant in each cubic foot of soil. When the grass grew green he hatched. When Greengrass set in, he pounced. But for him, 1937 would have been a bumper year. Wheat that was not eaten by grasshoppers was attacked by rust. Hay that would have made a ton and a half to the acre was thinned and chopped down in wanton waste. A single hopper could destroy ten times what he actually consumed.

I had Mindum Durum wheat, which was immune to

rust, and I had planted it on the "summer fallow" for which I had been so handsomely paid. Some time during the previous summer the corn had sprouted and died, leaving a weedless expanse covered with loose dust. The indolent hopper preferred to back into a crack in the ground to lay his eggs. Such cracks were to be found in the grassland but not on my summer fallow. The wheat therefore got a head start, and the hoppers that attacked it had to move in from surrounding soil.

I got out the binder and raced them for it. They got four or five bushels to the acre and I got fourteen. When the threshing machine pulled out of the field it left behind it three heaping stacks of straw. But while my plowed acres turned in these tonnages, the unplowed haymeadows yielded only three stacks of hay. I owed my survival to the plow.

In the fall another enemy appeared within my land. He was known in banking circles as a "float buyer" and the slow train service across South Dakota was his stock in trade. A float buyer could purchase a load of livestock on Saturday after the banks were closed, and hand the seller a rubber check. He could then ship the stock to terminal market and receive payment for it by Monday afternoon. Meanwhile his worthless check would not be presented at the local bank until Monday morning, and thereafter would have to journey by slow train service before it could be presented at its home bank. This mail-car financing, though the lapse of time was brief, enabled a smart buyer to buy and sell livestock without having any money. On a rising market, float buyers could ride to glory mounted on their fountain pens, with no one any the wiser.

In '37 there was a rising market. Minnesota farmers harvested a bumper crop of cheap grain. They turned to lamb feeding as an outlet for their product, and they were eager buyers. Dakota ranchers, on the other hand were discouraged sellers whose desperation made them snatch at offers which were not quite as high as the market justified. As a consequence, scalpers and commission men perched on our corral fences like buzzards, and the scratching of fountain pens was heard in the land.

Early in the season I had contracted my lambs to such a buyer. I asked eight and a half cents, he talked me down to eight and a quarter cents, gave me a check for a down-payment, and departed. The check was good.

When I reported the sale to my banker he warned me sternly to wire for confirmation on the final payment. He said that float buying was getting out of hand, and that someone was going to get hurt.

The hazards of this operation were not imaginary. Had the market fallen at any point, it would have required months of legal red tape to re-establish ownership of the livestock. Convinced of the wisdom of his advice, I warned the buyer that I was going to have confirmation before the lambs became his property.

The presence of all this phony money began to have an inflationary effect on values. Legitimate buyers who had come from Minnesota in person to fill their feedlots, were forced to higher levels by the float men, who in turn were encouraged to even greater boldness. By the time my delivery date arrived, I had to refuse offers of ten cents.

I was not happy about this paper loss, and the more inclined to be firm in my request that the check be confirmed by telegram before the lambs were loaded.

The psychological pressure that was brought to bear upon me was terrific. As the train idled on the track, and the lambs stood in the alley waiting to be loaded, it became increasingly apparent that I was a grasping, suspicious, and avaricious heel. The buyer who had given me the check and had presumably wired for the confirmation was utterly nonplused at the delay in the return telegram. The engine huffed and puffed, everyone was waiting — not for the telegram — but for me to surrender.

I couldn't do it. "Well," I said, "if you can't pay for these lambs, I've got another offer here at ten cents. I'll give you another half hour."

This brought action. The buyer hastened away, ostensibly to send another wire, but actually to get in touch with another scalper who had just completed a successful deal and had a little money. My check was OK'd by its home bank. The lambs belonged to the scalper, but the train had gone.

That afternoon the yards were quarantined for "scab." A load of sheep had come through suffering from that disease. A blanket quarantine was slapped on the whole state and a flurry of bad checks fluttered down to earth like so many autumn leaves. Several men went to jail, several neighbors lost their livestock to the legal profession, and the scratching of float buyers' fountain pens ceased to be heard in the land.

As I appraised my returns from the roller coaster year, I discovered that I had neither won nor lost — I had merely gotten my chips back. The tide of plenty had not recouped my '36 loss, it had merely granted me the right to gamble another year. And as the spring of '38 moved in to take up the task at which 1937 had failed, I discovered that my banker was looking down his nose at my paper.

"Your loan is getting a little top-heavy," he said.

I couldn't see why. I hadn't bought any sport roadsters and I had been rolling my own cigarettes out of cheap tobacco. Somewhere along the line Dakota had been picking my pockets again.

Chapter XV

SMALL MAN

SINCE 1930 I had come to look upon my persistent failures as bad luck. The Dust Bowl seemed to be a roulette wheel which no one could beat, and by 1938 it was very thinly played.

Houses were boarded up and abandoned. Trees along the banks of the prairie streams were dying with the death throes of the streams that watered them. Alfalfa fields whose roots had gone down thirty feet to hidden springs below the surface were giving up the ghost. There seemed to be every reason to commiserate with myself and curse my luck. Yet a few of my neighbors on land no better than my own were making money. Like me, they were growing sorghum cane which grasshoppers wouldn't eat, but unlike me they were buying and selling livestock, not raising it.

My banker expected me to make money. He didn't care how.

This frigid financial atmosphere caused me to question my formula. Could it be that I erred in assuming that this was roulette? Perhaps it was stud poker, a game in which it was sometimes wise to throw in a hand?

A MAN FROM SOUTH DAKOTA

Some of my neighbors were running their ranches so that they could, if they wished, throw in a hand.

I needed perspective.

I went fishing.

The beaver dam where I had once caught a two pound trout was no longer alive. The beaver had cleared out the aspen in a wide circle around it and had moved elsewhere. Without their care, flash floods had carried the dam away, and what had once been a deep pool, mysterious with the opal tinge of depth, was now a raw patch of silt through which a diminished stream ran in a thin trickle.

But while other trout streams were dead, and this creek was dying, one stream remained a law unto itself — the upper Spearfish. In better times, when the flood-muddied waters of spring had made fishing elsewhere a waste of time, I had gone to the upper Spearfish, for no rain or cloudburst had ever succeeded in carrying mud into the stream through the mat of moss and spruce needles that covered its watershed. Now, in bad times, drought had not varied its flow by so much as a cupful. There were no two pound trout, but I caught a basket full of small ones.

On the way home the ranching scheme that I studied was one aimed at small fish rather than large ones.

I could take it for granted, I felt sure, that the tide of good and bad years would continue to flow according to the ponderous rhythm they had followed up to now. I knew where I had failed — I had permitted my overhead to continue undiminished through years when my acres were in a stingy mood. I had kept men on the payroll when there wasn't enough work for them to do. I had kept my band of breeding ewes at all costs. When they had needed grass I had bought it for them, at any cost. I had been proud of hanging on, yet the fact remained that in '31, '34 and '36, I could have given them away and had more money left than I had made by hanging on.

In the spring of '37 I saw a neighbor sell his herd of stock cows and replace them with calves. One day I asked him why he had done it, and how he could make money on such a deal.

"A calf," he said, "will grow into money if you give him time. And if the year blows up and you haven't got the grass, you can sell him for what he cost. But if you have a wet cow the same year with a suckling calf, you can't *give* her away when no one has grass. I want calves because I can turn them quick if things go wrong."

It had taken me a year to translate that wisdom into sheep language. And when I approached my banker with this proposition he agreed that I was on the right track. But I had seen it a year too late.

When we tried to agree on the figure that my indebtedness would reach by shearing time of 1939, we couldn't see eye to eye. I thought it would cost me a thousand dollars to winter. He said that it would have to cost me less than six hundred — that was the most he could let me have. I said that at a thousand dollars I wouldn't be bathing in champagne. He replied that five dollars a head was the

199

loan top which a bank examiner would approve. He suggested that I get a loan from the FSA.

The FSA was a government agency designed to resettle destitute farmers on their land. The loans were tailored for financial cripples like myself. They didn't have to make any sense from the standpoint of security, nor did the man who acquired one have to worry about how he spent the money, for a supervisor would spend all the money for him. Every check had to be initialed by the supervisor. I didn't like it, but I wanted to stay in business.

In preparation for my interview I shaved and put on a pair of pants that had been pressed recently. But the men who were standing in line in the office when I arrived understood these matters better than I. They had left their whiskers untouched for a full week in preparation for their interview, they had kept their overalls out of the laundry for several weeks and had spent the intervening time in preparing their tales of woe. I listened to three — everything in this office was very public — and the tales had been well prepared.

When my turn came I advanced a proposition which I thought would pay out and put me in the clear in two years. I told the man that I had sixty tons of cane in the shock, that what I wanted to do was sell my old ewes, keep my ewe lambs, and buy more ewe lambs. I pointed out that the lambs could winter on cane and the the kind of grazing I had for them, and gain in value by the time I was ready to market them for yearling ewes. I could continue this process year after year, and when the rains came back I'd be ready to start with my own band of yearling ewes.

It was a plan moulded to the mood of this long thought that Dakota was thinking. A yearling ewe was the closest thing to a camel that could thrive in my latitude. If anything would pay out, this would pay out.

But the supervisor wasn't looking for plans that would pay out, he was looking for plans that wouldn't. He waited in vain for my tale of woe. I didn't have one ready. My wife didn't need an operation, I didn't have a wife; and none of my fourteen children were pining for food. I had been remembered by good fortune too recently, as evidenced by the crease in my pants. He said that the FSA only loaned to men who couldn't get credit elsewhere.

It looked like a six hundred dollar winter. I went back to the bank. "What do I have to do to keep out of that FSA Poor Farm?" I asked.

The banker gave me the arithmetic cold. If I could buy ewe lambs at four dollars a head and run my ranch for six months at a total expenditure of a hundred a month, I could keep out of the FSA Poor Farm.

So I drove several hundred miles that fall in search of widows and orphans whose throats I could cut for ewe lambs at four dollars. The price was barely within reach of possibility, for the current market was six cents a pound and I had to find light lambs or I couldn't afford them. I grew hump shouldered from looking over corral fences at lambs I didn't dare bid on because they were too heavy, and when my eye for weight betrayed me at the scales, I had to drive again to find enough "little dogs" to make my deal solvent.

When I had completed my purchases I had a corral full of lambs at three dollars and eighty-five cents. The last package of runts that I had found had enabled me to undercut the four dollar figure but beauty was not in them. They were such sorry looking creatures that I thought it best to use them as a proving ground for my sixty tons of cane.

I knew that cane grown in drought years could be poisonous. The "little dogs" ate it and lived. I decided that my cane wasn't poisonous.

The next morning, as snow swirled around my buildings, I held the whole band in the corral and gave them a feed of cane. Five minutes later nine of them were dead. At least thirty more were in convulsions. I dogged them out of the corral on the run and raked the ground with a garden rake until no shred of the deadly stuff was left. Three more died in the other corral while I was doing it.

I consulted a veterinary over the phone and was told that the snow and wet had released the prussic acid in my cane. I would have to wait for a deep freeze, he said, and even then must proceed with caution.

The hard freeze came, and with fear and trembling I tried the feed again. The lambs fell on it with gusto, the corral was literally alive with stalks of it being waved in the air. I stood over them for an hour, until at last they began to lie down and chew their cuds. None died.

Every day I took them out to grass when the weather permitted, and fed the cane only when blizzards raged. Every night I pored over the band from the vantage point of the corral fence, recalling where I had acquired certain individuals and what price I had paid. I saw that the big lambs were getting bigger, but the little dogs remained the same.

In the shearing pen I saw the same thing happen — the most expensive lambs were the cheapest in the end. Though Greengrass had been meager and badly gnawed by grasshoppers, the ewe lambs showed no ill effects from the daily chase for green shoots. They put on weight and wool and the wool check met on the nose my commitment at the bank.

One day a commission man came by and told me he thought he could get seven dollars a head for my yearling ewes for delivery in the fall.

"And," he added, "I know where you can contract a thousand lambs right now to fill your corrals again when you sell these."

The chase of the fall before was fresh in my mind, and I knew that in the fall the hunt for ewe lambs would be on in earnest. But a thousand lambs would take a lot of money, and the yearlings were not sold.

"I can't use anything but ewe lambs," I said. "What will I do with the five hundred wethers?"

"Sell 'em again, and buy five hundred more on contract the same way. You can shake the deal down to seven hundred and fifty ewe lambs when we're done dealing in the fall."

There was risk in the venture. I would have to borrow a thousand dollars now, and at least four thousand more on the delivery date. My feed supplies were a question mark and the seven dollars price on the yearlings was only conversation money.

"Let's go look at them," he urged me.

We drove sixty miles, with grasshoppers splashing on the windshield all the way.

I saw the lambs, and I wanted them, but I also wanted a million dollars.

The grower needed the downpayment and the commission man needed his commission. I needed the lambs. We circled them.

"All right," I said, "if the bank will go along, I'll take 'em."

As the summer wore on, and no rain fell, I became alarmed about a market for my yearling ewes. It began to look as though I might end by owning seventeen hundred sheep.

But one day a buyer appeared. He was a shrewd-eyed sheepman who looked every ewe in the eye and in the mouth. He took it for granted that I was a throat-cutting crook and he didn't believe anything I told him.

"I'll give you seven dollars a head for three hundred topped out of that bunch," he said at last.

"Nothing doing," I replied. "You can take three hundred as they come out of the chute at seven dollars. It will cost you seven twenty-five to sort them."

He accepted. For an hour and a half he chiseled and dug his way through the band, throwing out blackfaces, wool blinds, fuzzies, limpers, and parrot mouths. When he was through he had the best three hundred sheep in the band.

I had a bunch of culls, and I wasn't sure that anyone would ever want them. But two days later the FSA Supervisor arrived with one of his financial patients in tow.

The customer himself had apparently never seen a sheep before, but the Supervisor knew a great deal about them.

"Fine bunch of yearlings you've got there," he said.

I eyed him sharply in search of sarcasm, but I saw that he was in earnest. As he talked, and I listened, I realized that I was listening to a man who was proving that he had read the text, and who was about to spend some money that had cost him nothing in shoveling coal into engines or husking corn.

"How much do you want for them?" he asked.

Quickly I adjusted the price to fit the situation.

"Nine dollars a head," I said, "gate cut."

"OK," he said, "we'll take them all." And turning to his patient he said, "You can't go wrong on a bunch of stuff like that."

So the yearlings were gone and I had the money to pay for the lambs I had bought.

Meanwhile the commission man, needing another commission, had sold the wether end of the thousand head, and had bought me another five hundred on the same terms. While he was thus engaged I bought twenty tons of shelled corn to supplement my straw stacks. Straw and corn and a little grass was all the feed I had, for the whole fifteen hundred acres had turned in less than five tons of cane and hay. The farmer had piled up a lot of straw that the sheepman now needed, and needed badly. My scalp fairly prickled at the risk I was taking in putting seven hundred and fifty head of sheep on a piece of ground that hadn't grown enough feed that year to feed ten head of cattle.

But I had no sooner received the new crop of lambs than Hitler moved into Poland. Lamb prices jumped, the corn I had bought increased sharply in value, and when the dust of my operation settled, I had money in the bank.

I had money in the bank despite the fact that the Dust Bowl was no less dusty than before. The productivity of my acres had sunk lower than it had ever been. The hoppers swarmed in tumbling hordes over everything they could digest.

I had lived by growing things they couldn't eat. I was learning to live in Dakota by the same means that the desert primrose had survived there — by learning to close my financial petals when the heat was on.

Chapter XVI

THAT WHICH HAS BEEN BEFORE

HITLER's advance into Poland had healed my ailing mortgage at the bank, but as spring came again, and Hitler swept into Holland, it was perfectly apparent that there was blood on the moon.

Aunt Ida and Uncle Harry and I sat around the breakfast table while the radio blared a steady outpouring of unwelcome tidings. We had hoped the dykes of Holland would be breached, the land flooded, and Hitler stopped. But the dykes had not been breached and Hitler had not been stopped. The nightmares we had dreamed at night were still real in the light of day. We endured the radio because we were afraid to turn it off.

A car pulled up in the yard. Uncle Harry looked out the window.

"Looks like shearers," he said.

The car was a road-battered Buick with a bed roll strapped across the top and a grindstone riding the front bumper. Four men got out of it.

A MAN FROM SOUTH DAKOTA

I had no shearing pens set up, my woolsacks had not been purchased yet, nor the strings to tie the fleeces. I wasn't ready to shear. But the grease was out in the wool, and a shearer in the hand was worth two north of the River. In the space of time it took the crew captain to reach the door, I had decided to shear.

We bargained briefly and their car went off toward the barn. Uncle Harry went to town to buy sacks and strings, I called a neighbor on the phone and asked him to come and help pen sheep. Then I rode out into the pasture to start the herder home with the sheep. By the time we had corralled the band and had cut off a hundred head, the shearers had set up their own pens, had unearthed a hank of last year's strings from a rafter, and were yelling for sheep.

We hazed our cut into the shearing barn and filled the pens. Each shearer promptly grabbed a ewe by a hind leg, dumped her on her back, plucked the shears from his soup can, and shearing was in progress.

The neighbor I had called arrived in a cloud of dust, and leaving him in charge of the pens, I hastened to collect the rest of the shearing necessities — sacking needle, branding paint, stencils, sacking string, a tub of water to soak the sacks so they would stick to the sacking ring.

By the time I had returned with the supplies, a heap of bright, clean fleeces had already accumulated in the wool pen.

"Sheep out!" a shearer bawled.

THAT WHICH HAS BEEN BEFORE

Hastily we branded the penful of shorn sheep. I opened the gate and the yearlings went clattering across the floor toward freedom, shy and nervous in their summer garb. We had no sooner refilled the pen than the other shearers demanded the same attention. By the time we had finished filling the pens, the tin roof over our heads had begun to pop and crack in the growing heat of advancing morning, sweat was pouring from us all in streams, and fleeces had begun to bulk alarmingly in the wool pen.

Outside the barn a car door slammed and Uncle Harry hastened in with the armload of sacks and strings.

"Hear any more news?" I asked him.

"Not the kind you want to hear," he said. "The Belgians have quit — the king ratted."

"The hell!" I said. Words completely failed to express my sickness of heart. It seemed to me that I couldn't take much more of this calamity, helpless to do anything about it.

"And here we sit," I said, "armed to the teeth with twelve old whippet tanks and some CCC trucks."

A shearer looked up. The clamor of the sheep in his pen had prevented him from hearing all of our conversation.

"How's the war coming?" he asked. "Where we sheared yesterday the radio was busted."

"They'd all ought to be busted," my neighbor put in, and he brought the shearer up to date.

"Sheep out!" a shearer bawled.

The wrangler branded the shorn sheep and turned them

out. I picked up a woolsack and climbed the ladder to the sacking platform. Rigging the sack on the ring, I dangled it down through the hole and dropped into it.

"Hit me," I said.

The wrangler threw fleeces up to me one at a time. I caught them in upstretched arms and worked them down past my body into the sack. Through the burlap walls I heard the conversation continuing.

"Oh well," a shearer said, "the Dutch wasn't nothing, and the Belgians wasn't much, wait till they hit the French, then they'll find out something."

"I'd like to think so," said the wrangler, "but I ain't got any confidence in it. I got a feeling we ought to be over there."

"Not on your life!" the shearer said emphatically. "Lindbergh's got the right of it. We won a war for 'em once and got kicked for it. What I say is, let's stay home and mind our own business."

It was familiar ground. Woodrow Wilson and Teddy Roosevelt. Who was to decide? Everyone in that barn held a violent opinion on one side or the other, and wanted to shout it loud enough to drown other opinions out. I shared this temptation. But my opinion was too complex to be condensed readily into a single shout or a rubber stamp. It was harder to defend a belief in knowledge, or to wax sentimental over that straggling line of students who shuffled up Sixth Street every morning, convinced that they were slaves. It was difficult to answer a man who said the New Deal was a dictatorship and why fight for it, when I myself disapproved of it and thought that it was regimentation. It was confusing that the man whom I had doubted and disliked from the moment of his nomination was, almost alone, the champion of the course I favored, while the names I had once praised now trumpeted isolation.

The wool crowded me out of the sack. I sewed it shut with twine and dropped it to the shearing floor. This thing that was happening now had happened before. There had been high prices, and for those who were smart, there had been Buicks on the moon. Perhaps Dakota would also grant another 1916?

Chapter XVII

THAT WHICH IS DONE

DAKOTA had been thinking a long thought, and writing a long sentence. In the fall of '39 it achieved a punctuation mark, but I was standing so close that I couldn't tell whether it was a comma, a period, or a new paragraph.

While Frenchmen manned their Maginot Line, and English prepared to repel a human enemy from their land, an inhuman enemy departed from mine. The movement began as the grasshoppers took short flights from one field to another. They were thirsty and they were bored with the desolation they themselves had wrought. Suddenly the air was filled with them to a great height. Their silvered bodies glistened in the sun, and one could peer up into the blue sky and see them circling there as far as the eye could reach. In three days they were gone, and my tawny hills lay gaunt and drab beneath a warm fall sun. Untenanted now, my soil lay covered with a thin stand of old grass, dotted at wide intervals by the weathered gray bulk of the straw stacks which were the only visible increment from ten years on this land.

THAT WHICH IS DONE

By spring of 1940 there was no mistaking the change in Dakota's mood. During the Dust Bowl years, the clouds had faltered long on the sky line and then slowly limped away. Now they appeared swiftly, swept down without hesitation and rained. Following the first onslaught of the showers, more clouds moved in and what had begun as a cloudburst continued as steady rain.

I had a feeling as I watched the season unfold that I had come this way before. The weather was repeating itself, and many times the memory of old years prepared me in advance for situations before they arose. For one thing I could be sure that it was no season in which to mow a hundred acres before I stacked. Far better to lay down a single stack, take off the mower, put on the sweep, stack, though the change cost half an hour's work.

During the drought, sunflowers had encroached on some of my hay meadows. Cut early they would make good hay, but they ripened swiftly and once ripe were little better than brushwood. I was constantly faced with the necessity for choosing between one field and another, knowing when I chose the one that the other would escape me. I arose earlier and earlier in the morning, trying vainly to capture it all.

Following an old, familiar sequence, brand new events clamored for my attention. . . .

. . . weeds were gaining on the corn. . . .

. . . a book I had written came back from a publisher with a request for an immediate revision. . . .

. . . seated on the tractor, doing Dakota's bidding, I sought with longing the time for revision. . . .

. . . the second cutting of alfalfa was coming up through the first crop. . . .

. . . the wheat was getting ripe. . . .

. . . the binder fired bundles like a machine gun. . . .

. . . wheat was going to the bottom of the ocean and wheat would be very high in price. . . .

. . . while a family of Indians shocked the wheat and I ran a bundle wagon in a neighbor's field, Uncle Harry took Aunt Ida to the hospital with a persistent pain. . . .

. . . while Aunt Ida rested in the hospital and medical opinion hesitated short of surgery, I scooped grain into a neighbor's bin, thereby earning his services in my fields when the time came. . . .

. . . when we were nearing the end of the first day's threshing in my wheat, Uncle Harry drove in from town and plucked me from the job. The doctors were going to operate at midnight, there were no special nurses, both of us would be needed to help with the nursing during the first crucial night. . . .

. . . at two in the morning she cried out, "Oh Harry! Harry, help me!". . .

. . . he couldn't help her, but I could help him, and the man who had become my father became my son.

The next morning the neighbors, unaware of what had happened, came with their teams to thresh. The field we had been working in had not been shocked, it lay wide open to a rain, and Dakota was bringing up a cloud below the sky line. We held a hushed conference on the back steps and the neighbors went to the field to finish the patch.

Throughout the day, as people came and went, the men and the teams who had worked in the field yesterday, worked in the field today. In midafternoon they finished the unshocked grain and the machine, out of respect for the dead, left the shocked fields unthreshed and moved on to the next ranch.

A month later the threshing machine came back and the land took hold of us again.

Its hold was strengthened by our need for it, and by its insistence upon our attention. There was too much grain to be gleaned from fields for our small band of sheep to salvage, there was too much hay in the stack to insist upon a continuation of our yearling deal. It was now time to keep our yearlings — the rain had come back.

The next spring I wrote to a friend: "Lambing was a tiger this year, but thanks to our new Ford Ferguson tractor, we got the job done, and I never saw more mud in all my life. From the time we started until we finished we had nine inches of moisture, most of it in wet snowstorms. There was no bottom to the prairie and cars and trucks couldn't get anywhere. But this bowlegged Ford doesn't interfere with itself and goes anywhere, any time, pulling a trailer back of it. . . .

A MAN FROM SOUTH DAKOTA

"This kind of a spring a herder has to have good strong pelvic sockets to keep from leaving his legs behind him in the mud, but this year I put the herder on the tractor in the morning, and as fast as lambs came he loaded them under the tent on the "gutwagon." When he had six ewes and their lambs in the gutwagon, he came home to the barn with it at twelve miles an hour, unloaded and went back a mile and a half in less than twenty minutes for the round trip. . . .

"I used the same outfit at night at the corral. My corrals were fishponds and my barn was a cesspool, one corral was eighteen inches deep in mud. But I fenced a well drained side hill before we started to lamb. I'd never been able to use that ground before because it was too far away from the barn to drag a ewe. If you've ever tried to straddle a ewe and strongarm her down a slippery side hill while you've got a pair of twins draped over one arm, you'll know what I mean. But with Little Joe and the Gutwagon I backed up to the gate and stood there in the tent out of the rain until I heard a ewe talking baby talk. I'd grab her by the lapels, hustle her into the tent, let her lamb there on dry straw, and when I had a load I turned on the lights and ferried them across the fishponds to the barn. Little Joe was a saddle horse, a clubhouse for the herder, a taxi, and an amphibian barn. . . .

"We finished lambing the 21st of May and when the fields were dry enough, we went back at the farming. We disced, drilled and dragged seventy-three acres of oats in less than a week, then went on plowing for flax. All told we've broken a hundred and fifty acres of go-back sod for flax, on top of planting a hundred and fifty acres of small grain. . . .

"We sheared three days ago and today I've been excavating up on the hill where my dipping outfit went down under the dust. I found it about two feet down, and tomorrow we're going to dip. . . ."

Two good years in a row. The Dust Bowl and the tom-tom beat were dead. Dakota was thinking another kind of thought.

The prophets of weather who had peered at the sun and predicted a repetition of the wet and abundant twenties, had accurately called the turn. The pattern of those years was being repeated.

But if the sun had been able to return the compliment, and had possessed the curiosity to study Dakota, where its whims had been so long dominant, not only would it have seen a small, token horde of buffalo which had been snatched from extinction by human hands, but it would have seen another horde of weird, migrant monsters which had replaced the buffalo.

Rubber tired tractors running at speeds of thirty miles per hour, hauled sixteen foot combines the full length of the Great Plains every summer. They raced southward in the spring and began to gnaw their way northward from Texas to the Canadian line. There were fewer straw stacks, and the taller stubble left by the monsters was plowed back into the land.

There was now financial self-respect where always before farming had meant financial indignity. The word "surplus" was dead, increased acreages were not only invited by the desire for profit, they were planted in answer to patriotic pleas.

Government was now talking from another book, pleading for more acres under cultivation, for more little pigs, and was guaranteeing a handsome price. At the same time, Dakota was giving every acre that was plowed the rain it needed to make a crop.

But Government was still Government, and Dakota was still Dakota.

Government worked men forty hour weeks in munitions plants and Dakota worked one-hundred-and-ninety-six hours a week, ripening hay and grain, and hailing fields into a pulp at regular intervals.

The tonnages we handled and the ponderous might of the forces we opposed dwarfed the arithmetic of the munitions industry. An inch of rain on an acre of land is twenty-seven hundred tons of water. Multiplied by ten (as sometimes happened in a hailstorm or cloudburst) and sent rushing down a draw, it could rip forty square miles of crop to shreds and wreck a hundred miles of fence. Dakota could put twenty-four inches of snow on the ground, add zero cold and a forty mile wind, and our outposts became as isolated as the North Pole. We were at war also, but for the most part we fought alone, with skeleton crews and sometimes with skeletons for crews.

Government asked us to increase our tonnages. Once we had planned them, we were committed to handle them when the time came, whether we had men or not. Compared with the tons of battleships and tanks and planes, our scoopfulls and bucketfuls and forkfuls were still respectable. But we didn't have enough men, we couldn't buy machines, so we had to learn to make machines.

When a workman in a tank factory was discovering that sprockets for tanks could be cut with an acetylene torch, four at a time, my hired man was dreaming up a grain elevator from the the wreckage of an old threshing machine, and with it we put five thousand bushels of wheat and flax in our bins without bending our backs. I stretched a mile of flood-tangled sheepwire with the tractor, pulled posts with its hydraulic lift, made it a nursemaid during lambing, put lights on it so that it could keep pace with Dakota's hours. Between the demands of War, and those of Dakota, a Dakotan had to become a mechanic, or come apart at the seams.

But it was a good game, and it seemed — on the face of it— to be a better game than roulette. The latter we also played, and the gambling dens on Main Street in Deadwood Gulch, upon which I had once looked down as a child, were occasionally viewed by us from the inside.

"What number are you going to throw next, Ed?" Uncle

219

Harry inquired one evening, knowing that the question would goad the dealer into vigorous denial.

"If I knew that, I could make a million dollars," Ed lied.

"How do you like seventeen?" Uncle Harry insisted.

"Seventeen is a good number," Ed said placidly. "They're all good numbers — if they come."

So Uncle Harry played seventeen and thirty-four came. . . .

The other gamble looked better. We had two carloads of lambs that fall, and because the "feeder" lamb price was low, and the price of "fats" was high, I put them in the corral and tried my hand at "feeding them out." And so, the time that I had planned to spend on the long delayed revision of the book, I spent instead looking over a corral fence, watching for signs of founder and other feedlot ailments.

Uncle Harry went down to market with the shipment of lambs, and came home beaming. "You should have seen those Iowa feeders lining up to bid on that pen of lambs!" he said. "Too bad we didn't have enough grain to finish them out. Maybe next year we should plant more."

I looked over the well thumbed letter that the publisher had written to my agent months before. ". . . . after years of hard times he seems to be well on his way to becoming a successful farmer, and, I suspect, a successful author. I'll be glad to go over the manuscript with him a chapter at a time, if he desires. . . ."

I was tired of penning excuses. I laid the matter away to

rest, once and for all saying quite truthfully that writing was a luxury I couldn't afford. I felt older and wiser than the teacher of creative writing who, sixteen years before, had told me that before I could write anything, I must first be something. Being something seemed to be answer enough. A man might conquer the public taste for a time, and in the midst of fame, have fame grow tasteless in his mouth. But here was an opponent who would never tire, who always offered something new to imperil — and improve — the flavor of next year.

Chapter XVIII

DAKOTA BEACHHEAD

SHEEP RANCHING, I had long since discovered, was like eating spaghetti — there was no clear cut line of division between the bites. But if there was any day in the year more crucial than the rest, it was the day on which a sheepman opened the gate of his buckpen. Flipping that gatehook was the capital letter of a new sentence.

The bucks were more than willing that I should turn them out. Smooth and vigorous from long graining, they bristled about their prison, fighting among themselves, slamming the wall with their horns, demonstrating their masculinity.

I had always been trigger-happy with the buckpen. It was somehow gratifying to release that tide of vitality upon the quiet surface of a band of ewes. Like water running down hill, like fire sweeping through dry grass, this irrevocable rite would churn the whole herd into a turbulent activity. Within a matter of seconds there would be twenty simultaneous matings, then twenty more. Five months later there would be lambs, in the same order; and they would come in that order and in those numbers no matter what Dakota's mood might be at the time.

For eighteen seasons I had been trying to outguess Dakota's mood five months in advance, and every year, when the lambs began to drop, I had found good reason to curse the date of my choice. Either mud, or bitter cold, or drought-seared grazing had made me wish that I had chosen a period earlier or later, or had birth-controlled the whole affair.

Now my nineteenth lambing season was coming up. It was certain to face a labor market completely stripped of all seasonal help, a weather cycle which promised mud or snow or both, and the niggardly rationing of everything I would need, from gasoline to coffee, from lumber to flashlight batteries. A March lambing would cut my labor needs in half, and carpentry — if I could find the time and the lumber — could take the place of human labor.

But carpentry hadn't been too successful in a March lambing just a year earlier. Somehow I had never found the time to repair the hole that a trucker had smashed in a corner of the barn, or to seal the cracks that time and weather had made in the siding, and it still wasn't done when a vicious blizzard ushered in the lambing season with a seventy mile wind and temperatures of fifteen below. The wind had chased the cold through every crack in the barn wall, and not even the body heat of seven hundred ewes could raise the thermometer to zero. New lambs froze stiff before their mothers got up to care for them. But if we caught the lamb on the first bounce and rushed it to a brooder stove to dry it off, the ewe wouldn't claim it an hour later. An unclaimed lamb didn't last long by either route. The first two mornings my elderly hired man went cheerfully down the rows of pens spinning dead lambs out into the alleyways as nonchalantly as though they were old picnic plates.

Belatedly we remembered the lambing tents ordinarily used for prairie lambing, and throughout the next forty-eight hours of the storm we tented everything before it came, shoving the tent pegs down into the manure of the barn floor, and banking the tents with straw. The canvas held the ewe's body heat as well as that of the steaming birth fluids and the heavy losses ceased. Eventually we docked an eighty per cent crop, which meant that March lambing had been better than the previous May lambing by a scant five per cent. It was a Hobson's choice — a lamb seemed to freeze just as dead in a cold rain as he did at fifteen below.

As I stood there fingering the gate hook, I didn't like the looks of any lambing date I could think of. But at least one element of certainty urged a March lambing. Two bachelor sheepmen, neighbors of mine, needed some field tillage that my tractor could do and theirs couldn't. They offered to trade help if I would work their fields in the fall, one of them would help me lamb, if I lambed in March. Neither could leave their own business in February or April. I didn't like March. Nor April. Nor February. Better perhaps to lamb all seven hundred head the Fourth of July?

I pulled my mind back to March. It was only six months since I had made myself some solemn promises as to how I would conduct a March lambing next time. Next year I would plug every hole in the barn before the winter even got started, and next year I would build enough extra lambing pens so that I would never have to evict a family before it was ready to go. Wool-blind ewes, and ewes with cockleburs lodged in the wool near the udders had always cost me disowned lambs. Next year I would get a shearing crew in to tag the band, and shear out the eyes in the same operation. Now I looked at these promises and couldn't see for the life of me why they couldn't be kept. If they *were* kept, how could weather touch me?

I flipped the gate hook.

Throughout a mild November and December I hauled hay every day that I could get at it, trying to get the lofts full against the time when lambs would be dropping. I approached the agent of the Commodity Credit Corporation about the possibility of buying some of the stored wheat I held on the place, and learned that the wheat I had sold for a dollar thirty-two a bushel I could buy back for a dollar seven. I therefore set the feed bunks in rows near the government bin and began to ladle wheat to the sheep earlier than usual because wheat is too heavy a feed for breeding ewes until they have become accustomed to it, and I didn't want to leave their wool hanging on the corral fence. I made a deal with a shearing crew to tag the band "sometime in February," and went over the hill to the neighbors' for four days to earn my March lambing help.

Under the pressure of these additional jobs, the task of hauling hay and repairing the barn moved very slowly. I was herding and hauling at the same time; I was pitching hay into the barn and mowing it back at the same time. Two loads a day was a good day. As December moved along toward Christmas I had two lofts jammed and a third one half full, but I found no time to plug up the holes in the barn which had cost me lambs the year before.

Then I found a man. I thought I had seen everything in the way of hired help, but Walter Carson was something new under the sun. A man in his middle fifties, he was as prim as a maiden aunt. He shaved every morning, his face glistened with soap and lotions, his old-model car shone with attention and care. After every meal he retired to his bunk house for twenty minutes to chank raw carrots a measured number of chanks, for their vitamin content. Nothing quite like him had ever been seen before on Dakota land.

I owed his presence on mine to the fact that he had promised the Deputy Collector of Internal Revenue that he wouldn't earn more than one hundred dollars a month and board in 1943, and his income had exceeded it. He accepted my offer of seventy-five a month and board in order to tidy up his income tax. But he was fully aware that he was working too cheap, and he had no intention of delivering more than seventy-five dollars' worth of muscle per month. He measured his effort to fit his wage, and put in his spare time studying a book which contained detailed information on how to live despite the occult influences of the signs of the moon.

As we proceeded with the business of hauling hay, Walter struggled to save me from my ignorance. I learned that a cow bred in a certain quarter of the moon will invariably produce a bull calf. I learned that alfalfa planted in the wrong quarter of the moon will never produce seed. So closely was he linked with the moon in my mind that under my breath I began thinking of him as "Mullins" and in a very short time I completely forgot his last name, which may or may not have been Carson.

Twenty years earlier I would probably have jumped down Mullins' throat in the interest of scientific truth, but I had lost some of my earlier enthusiasm for missionary work and I maintained a discreet silence. But as time passed, my noncommittal grunts aroused the suspicion in Mullins that I was a heretic, and he began to deliver his lecture with the injured air of one who casts pearls before swine.

"Walter," I said, at last, "I think I'll have you work on the barn. Take a hammer and nails and fix that wall so you can't see a crack of daylight inside of it. I mean windows and all. When the barn is pitch dark inside, we'll cut some new windows. Meanwhile, as long as you can see a pinhole of light anywhere, you aren't done yet."

"What about the hay?" he asked.

"The barn is more important right now," I dissembled. "You work on that and I'll haul hay."

He nodded and went to work. While I hauled hay, he banged on the barn, a measured number of bangs per nail.

When the barn was full of hay, I joined Mullins in his hammering. We plugged every hole, sealed every crack; we built extra lambing pens and fitted them into corners ready for occupancy. By the last week in January we were completely ready for a March lambing.

Then on January 27 Dakota opened its maw and took a big, long bite at my hay.

Two months later, when I collected my bale of daily papers at the newspaper office, it was possible to see, almost at a glance, how big and how wide that bite had been. The headlines of those two months fell into place as neatly as a row of dominoes:

WEST RIVER DIGS OUT FROM GREATEST STORM IN YEARS

JAN. 28. Black Hills' residents burrowed out of their homes today after the worst storm in 15 years had paralyzed all traffic, closed schools, clogged telephone communications and taken one life.

The storm, which struck with relentless fury early Thursday morning, began to wear itself out late in the afternoon. Twenty-three inches of snow fell during the storm and was whipped by a high wind which rose in gusts to speeds of 70 miles an hour. . . .

228

DAKOTA BEACHHEAD

ENTIRE STATE SHIVERS
IN BELOW ZERO COLD

FEB. 11 The severest cold wave in nearly a year with temperatures to 31 below struck with a vengeance last light to underscore a winter that. . . .

NEW STORMS FORECAST
FOR SOUTH DAKOTA

THREE INCHES OF SNOW FALLS IN NORTHERN HILLS; LOW TEMPERATURES IN PROSPECT FOR ENTIRE STATE. . . .

ROTARY PLOWS TO OPEN
ROADS IN MEADE COUNTY

CONCERN FELT OVER SHORTAGE OF FEED IN ISOLATED AREAS: PROGRESS SLOW ON CLOGGED HIGHWAYS.

FEB. 19. A renewed offensive against clogged roads in Northern Meade County, where several ranching communities are now in the fourth week of isolation, was opened today . . .

. . . snowbanks, piled up by previous plowings of the road, are ten feet high in stretches, necessitating the use of a rotary to blow the snow over the banks and widen the highway . . .

. . . some concern has been felt for stockmen who went into the winter with inadequate feed supplies. The deep, heavily crusted snow makes grazing impossible, forcing ranchers to fall back on their grain and hay supplies. . . .

229

COLD WAVE, WIND AND SNOW
FORECAST FOR SOUTH DAKOTA

MARCH 11. Storm-mauled northwestern South Dakota is in for another pounding over the weekend, the weatherman said, after one day of moderate temperatures had given weather-weary farmers and ranchers a foretaste of spring.

Coming in on what appears to be a regular once-a-week schedule, the forecast storm will pull tighter the six-week-old blockage of the northwestern region. . . .

SNOW PLOW ARMADA
SENT TO WEST RIVER

PLIGHT OF ISOLATED RANCHERS
ACUTE—HIGHWAY 16 BLOCKED

LIVESTOCK FEED SITUATION CRITICAL

Ranchers Fear Severe Lamb Crop Losses Inevitable; Continued Severe Winds Keep Roads Closed.

MARCH 14. The situation of northwestern South Dakota ranchers, snowbound and short of feed, serious a week ago, is fast becoming critical. Where there is feed, ranchers cannot get to it. Some cattle and sheepmen have plenty of hay on their places, perhaps several miles from their homes, but are unable to reach it.

A battle against blocked roads was resumed today as the weatherman held out promise of clearing weather, after the area was released from the grip of

230

a storm that buffeted portions of the region for three straight days. . . .

The deep snow which fell Jan. 27 has melted but little and even should the weather turn warm or a chinook start a thaw it would probably go off so fast that the bottom would fall out of the roads. One truck and trailer was stuck for a day in a narrow cut, with the trailer stuck at the top. The driver dug all day from the top of his trailer before he could move on.

Winds have been so severe that the usual crust has not prevented drifting. Particles of ice have been whipped into the cuts along with loose snow, closing the roads time after time. . . .

PORTIONS OF
MAIN HIGHWAYS
BROKEN OPEN

*Fleet Of Plows Ordered To
Clear Country Roads In An
Effort To Relieve Ranchers
In Northern South Dakota*

MARCH 15. A large snowplow armada, thrown into the battle against blocked roads in northwestern South Dakota with orders to open quickly the barricaded country roads for the relief of farmers and stockmen, had today broken through portions of the main highway which were blocked by the weekend storm that rivalled the "big blow" of Jan. 26-27. . . .

Army equipment including rotaries, pushplows, bulldozers, and multiple wheel drive trucks has been ordered into the storm stricken area . . . . by

231

A MAN FROM SOUTH DAKOTA

Major General Clarence Danielson, commanding officer of the Seventh Service Command, at Omaha. . . .

COMMUNICATIONS WITH
SNOWBOUND AREA HAMPERED

Freezing Rain Falls over Isolated Territory; Few Reports Heard From Plow and Truck Crews.

MARCH 17. Several spearheads of a snow plow armada, thrown into action against the seven-week-long barricade of northwestern South Dakota, out of communication today with their headquarters, are proceeding today under the worst possible conditions.

The work is proceeding around the clock, despite the weather, which is again unfavorable today. "The snow has rendered the mechanical equipment on farms useless," Major Eustrom said in declaring, "it looks like we'll have to go back to the old methods of doing the work with horse and wagon. . . ."

PLOWS BREAK 14-FOOT
DRIFTS TO OPEN ROADS

MARCH 22. Scores of ranchers and farmers are slowly being released from an eight-week-long snow barricade in northwestern South Dakota by Army-State snow removal equipment, but machinery crackups and muddy roads are bringing new woes to struggling crews. . . .

DAKOTA BEACHHEAD

FIRST SNOW, NOW MUD DELAYS
LIBERATION OF ISOLATED
S. D. RANCHES. . . . .

. . . . NINTH WEEKLY STORM
STRIKES PRAIRIE AREA . . . .

. . . . COLD AIDS CREWS
ON MUDDY ROADS . . . .

NEW STORMS FORECAST
FOR SOUTH DAKOTA

MARCH 27. A brewing storm in north-western South Dakota, which snow removal crews have struggled for weeks to free from a snow blockade, threatened today to re-block much of the country that has been opened. . . .

SNOW PILES INTO NEWLY
OPENED DRIFTS AGAIN. . . .

. . . PLOW CREWS ORDERED
TO CONCENTRATE ON
CRITICAL AREAS

MARCH 30. . . . Most road outfits today awaited clearing weather before beginning again the. . . .

233

Once again I found it hard to fit this dramatic language to the realities I had just been experiencing myself, and I found myself resenting the implication that I personally had needed any help from the Army or the State or anyone else. If there had been any spearheads whistling around my countryside, none of them had sailed past my ear, and I had seen nothing of the Armada. My first reaction to the record was a disgusted snort.

But on sober reflection I had to confess to having undergone a parallel period of apprehension and self-sympathy. If this language had gone astray, it was hard to say at just what point it had done so. Certainly my own fear of feed shortage had been "acute."

The fear had set in less than a week after the storm period had begun. Looking at the naked boards of one empty hay loft, it was easy to visualize the other two lofts also empty, and to remember when the barn lofts had all been empty for two solid weeks and a hundred sheep had died. As the drifts remained intact, I fed a ton of hay a day from the lofts, and the hayrack, standing empty under the loft door, was buried under a ten foot drift that would cost at least an hour of shoveling. . . .

Within sight of the house, half a mile away, was the point of one ridge which the wind had succeeded in blowing clear. It was on another man's ground, a man who didn't like sheep, but my necessity recognized no such law of possession. With a grain pail I led the band through the shallow portions of the drifts, under my line fence, and onto the bared grassland. It was ringed on all sides by impassable drifts. I left the sheep there to herd themselves, knowing that they would faithfully follow their own trail homeward, and went home to puzzle over my "useless mechanical equipment."

The rubber-tired Ford wouldn't pull the big hayrack, it would only pull a small two-wheeled trailer, relatively no bigger than a baby buggy. The steel wheeled 15-30 would pull the hayrack, but couldn't be steered — the drifts would seize the front wheels, and any progress was made, half sideways, at a snail's pace.

But the little tractor would pull a miniature load over the snow from the stacks and leave a track that the front wheels of the clumsy 15-30 would follow. In this fashion we managed to get hay to the top of the hill above the barns. We spread some there against the time when winds would make it unsafe to send our band out to steal grass on the distant hilltop.

Then under the impact of another blizzard, and severe cold, the snowdrifts changed in texture. They became granular and the 15-30 lost its power over them. But, we learned, the rubber-tired trailer worked better on this footing. Furthermore, the narrow two-wheeled trailer could be pulled in the narrow clearings which the wind had blown around the stacks, and by making four fast trips with the little outfit, we could equal the capacity of the big rack.

The last week in February the shearing crew called from town.

"Do you still want to tag those sheep?" a voice said.

"When?" I asked. "I'm busy as hell right now, and I'm not so sure you can get out here."

"We can get out early in the morning when the roads are froze," was the reply.

I'd been planning to haul hay while the roads were frozen. I balanced the value of a load of hay against that of a tagged band.

"O. K." I said. "We'll be ready to go when you are."

By sundown the next afternoon I finished sacking two three hundred pound bags of tags, while my band stood around regarding one another with their newly raised eyebrows, and another blizzard chased the shearers over the hill.

Then the fear clamped down again — I had lost a day hauling hay, the first lamb had come, hastened a little perhaps by rough handling in the shearing pen, but the rest could not be far behind. It was getting to be that time of the month.

In the three days following we managed to fill the lofts before the lambing got into full swing. The "swing," when it happened, was something. I had been a little extravagant in graining my bucks throughout the period of their confinement. Because of the shortage of harvest help, I had been compelled to thresh my field of oats with the hay-sweep which meant that the ground near the threshing machine was piled with shattered grain, grain too badly mixed with rocks and gravel to put through the machine. I had loaded this into a wagon and had poured it into the bucks in order to "save" it. As a consequence of this diet, the daily lambing rate jumped from the forty-a-day upon which I usually counted, to fifty-a-day, with a heavy sprinkling of twins.

Lambs were dropping all over the place. I had twenty pens set up in the long shed and twenty-five more in odd corners, all full. The mothers had to be watered and fed hay, and lambs had to be checked to make sure they had received that all-important first feed. The main band still had to be watered and fed — from the loft. Ben hadn't shown up yet, and I couldn't spare Mullins to haul hay, or even trust him with the band while I was doing it. . . .

Ben came, walking the three miles which separated our ranches. He took one look at the hay situation and volunteered to go out with the big tractor after a load of hay. He was gone six hours. During that time I could hear the transmission howling as he lunged and rocked his load through the drifts. At length he showed up on top of the hill with a towering load of hay which he parked there for the night.

We took the band up to the hay on the hill the next morning, but the weather was rough and one of us had to stand over them at all times to anticipate births. When a ewe started to lamb we grabbed her and hustled her down to the barn.

Nevertheless, Ben and Mullins got through that day with

the go-cart and hauled eight loads of hay with the light tractor. As they came and went, unloading in the loft, I stood over the band on the hill and kept one jump ahead of the new arrivals.

Ben was out of snuff and Mullins was out of carrots. The coffee was gone, and since my coupons had all been swallowed by two night shifts in the lambing shed, I needed to get to town to find something to make our drinking water look black — Postum or some other coloring material. A trip to town was imperative, but with the hay situation as it was, and lambs dropping fifty a day, I couldn't quite see it.

The next day I ran out of smoking tobacco. Roads or no roads, lambs or no lambs, I had to get to town. So I went to town. I slammed the car down the road and filled it to the gunwhales with smoking, chewing, and eating supplies. I sandbagged a grocer for some coffee, black-marketed a slab of bacon, and set out for home.

Within two miles of home I ran into rolling mud. The wheels picked up the clay and collected it against the fenders and running gear. With the motor in low and the accelerator flat to the floor I could lunge ten feet before the motor died. After a dozen lunges the clutch quit with a dismal whine. I was stuck.

I walked home two miles, pausing every twenty steps to shake a cake of mud off my feet. I helped Mullins and Ben shed the sheep, then Ben and I went back on Little Joe and brought the groceries from the car.

From that point on we were without a car — the rolling mud froze solid that night.

We had no time to bemoan the fact that it was too stormy to haul hay. Within the warm cave of our barn there was enough work for six men. For ten days, lambs had been dropping, fifty and sixty a day and the barn was jammed with them. As those in the individual pens survived a brief trial with their mothers, they had to be turned out to make room for new arrivals. The upper end of the barn was taken over by small drops of lambs. We now had five hundred or more in these small bunches, and since the job of carrying water to them in pails would have been out of the question, we were forced to drive them out to water. The task of haying, graining, and watering the maternity wards alone took many hours, and in addition new lambs were arriving around the clock.

Mullins continued to measure his effort according to his wage. He delivered eight hours work and retired to his bunkhouse to munch carrots and reflect upon the intentions of the moon. Ben and I, more prodigal of our time, worked at any hour there was a job to be done. One of us was always on duty, sometimes we both worked all night, then stole back our sleep in two-hour snatches. As the storm roared by outside, we were secure behind our defenses, but we were becoming woefully overcrowded, and much depressed by the tenement conditions. In one pen alone we had confined forty twin-mothers and eighty lambs. We were so crowded that at length we were forced to turn these in with the others and drive them to water. Twins became separated, and we hauled out our first dead lambs.

Ben and I had just finished shoveling out the south door to get the ewes out to water, when we heard the sound of trains on the railroad ten miles away.

"I don't know about your place," said Ben, straightening up, "but when we can hear those trains at home, it's a sure sign of some weather cooking."

"It's the same here," I said. "We'd better make another stab at getting in some hay."

So we got our weather report several hours before the blizzard struck, and I took over the penning, while Ben went out with Big Joe.

Several hours later he slammed down through the drift above the barn with the 15-30 and a ton and a half of hay. We parked it in front of the barn and carried in the day's feed. The storm hit that night.

While "Plow Crews Concentrated on Critical Areas" the lambing rate dropped from fifty to ten and from ten to five. We were through lambing, and we had a week's supply of hay in the loft. The tide of fertility that I had released with the gate hook had safely reached shore. The barn was full of lambs, exactly how many it would be impossible to say until we had docked and counted the tails.

It was time for Ben to go home, but he was reluctant to leave until we had tallied our score. In the sheep business the lambing scoreboard is the tail count, which doesn't lie.

"Weather or no weather," Ben said, "let's dock 'em and see how we stack up."

I was willing, but Mullins spoke up, and in no uncertain terms.

"You can't dock those lambs today," he stated firmly.

"Why not?" I asked.

"The moon signs is wrong," he answered.

"Aw to hell with the moon signs!" I snorted. "Get in there and start catching lambs."

He glared at me for a moment, then his lips pursed in determination. He flung the hammer at my feet, unloaded his pocketful of nails, and marched off toward the house.

"Is Mullins quitting?" Ben asked.

"I don't know," I said, "but he doesn't seem to want that hammer any more."

"Well, let's get at it," Ben said. "I want to know. I've never seen a prettier lambing nor one when the weather was any worse."

Four hours later we counted the tails on a lambing crop that tallied out at one hundred and four per cent.

I was feeling pretty good — I'd never cracked a hundred per cent before.

"By God," Ben said, "we sure did everything right."

"Where do you get that 'we' stuff?" I said. "It was me that did it — I turned the bucks in at the right time of the moon."

Ben started toward me and I started to run. He ran me down, and picking me up in his arms like a sack of feathers, he stood me on my head in a lambing pen and went home.

I brushed myself off and went up to the house to find Uncle Harry grousing discontentedly over a heap of dirty dishes.

"Goddamit!" he burst out, before I could make my brag about the docking count, "why the hell don't you get married? I'm tired of washing dishes."

I took a drink from the water pail on the wash bench and caught a glimpse of my face in the mirror. There was gray in my hair, there was gray in my whiskers, and the lines that once had appeared on my face only when I came in out of the cold, had become permanent.

"I'm not a kid any longer," I said, "and what will happen to a woman I marry and bring to this goddam ranch when the time comes for *me* to come down in a pile?"

Chapter XIX

THE DEVIL AND ERIC SMEEL

NOT LONG after my bumper lamb crop had gone out to grass, I saw a sparrow fall. Eric Smeel, who had habitually lambed better than a hundred per cent when I was a boy, came down in a pile.

When I entered the church I was surprised to find the pews full and the altar heaped high with flowers. Eric had no family, but his neighbors had all come. As I took my seat in the quiet and regarded the silent coffin, the thought crossed my mind that Eric would have been flattered and pleased by all this attention. But I recognized at once that this was nonsense, for if Eric had been granted sufficient consciousness to appreciate his own funeral, his first thought would have been to escape it. He would have extricated himself from the funeral trappings and, limping up the aisle, would have hastened home to straighten out his bungled chores.

The silence continued, and it occurred to me that my chores also would one day go on without me.

The minister began his sermon. It was not concerned with Eric Smeel. Like an enterprising salesman with one

243

foot in a door the minister seized instead the opportunity to display the wares of the theory which he represented. He raised his voice and spoke of the Devil and the Good Life.

It soon became apparent that the minister had never seen the Devil. He had never looked up from his work with his eyes full of grit and dust to see the Devil standing there spraddle-legged above the black clouds of a dust storm, nor heard him say, "Do you surrender? Do you give up?" And he didn't know how hard it was to answer, "I won't surrender, I won't give up."

Eric knew, and he had never surrendered. True, he had at odd intervals surrendered to the minor imps that one meets in saloons. He liked women and whiskey and beer. But just as it appeared that he had lost all sense of direction, one would look up to find him staggering out the door, on his way home to his beloved chores.

For life paid Eric off in chores. He was always longer about them than any other man I ever saw. He made them last, because to him an eating sheep was handsome, or a well topped haystack, or a singing hen. Life gave him no big payments to mark down in his books. He had no wife, no sons, not much companionship except from his radio, and no big thoughts to keep him company while he ate his meals alone. Life paid him in small coin, and every night he tendered his receipt, saying contentedly, "Well, that's that."

But in the spring of 1927 the Devil came in person to

enter Eric's life. There was a flood on in the Mississippi Basin, a hundred people were perched on housetops in the Atchafalaya country. The Devil needed a head of water to wash them out to sea and he had come to our country to get it. He was getting it in the form of a steady, pouring rain.

Eric was in his barn at the time, shearing out ewes who had maggots because of the wet, green pasture. The Devil, angered by his cheery face, paused long enough to lay the first hot finger of pain on Eric's right hand.

Eric dropped his shears and felt his hand. He thought he'd sprained it. Or maybe it was rheumatism brought on by the rain? He couldn't tell, but the fact remained that he couldn't close the shears, and the maggots were still feeding on the flesh of his ewes. He came and asked me if I would shear them out, and I did so.

When haying time arrived, and the alfalfa meadows were jungles of hay, Eric could drive his mower and rake, but he couldn't handle a fork to haul and stack the hay. So for the first time since I had known him, Eric shared his work with another man.

The man was a flood sufferer from the Mississippi Basin who said that he had been flooded out so many times that he had quit and come north to see where all the water was coming from. He had a wife and five children and Eric kept them through the summer until he had cut all his grain and put up his hay. Then he let them go, because the size of his place didn't justify his keeping even one man.

He put a copper wire around his wrist to cure the rheumatism. It worked fine, he said. The currents in the copper stopped the pain. He was able to do his chores.

The copper wire worked all right until the winter of 1929, when the pain broke out in his hip, and there wasn't much of any way he could put copper around that. He decided it would be cheaper to spend some money getting a real cure. It was either that or hire a man all the time. So he went away for a week to a sanitarium where a fellow cured people just by touching them with his hands. He came back cured.

I didn't see Eric at all for a couple of years, except now and then on the streets in town. But I learned by the grapevine that he was having his hay put up by neighbors on shares, and that he had cut his band of ewes from a hundred down to fifty head.

It was in the summer of 1931 that he showed up at my place again.

"Have you got any barrels you could loan me to haul water in?" he asked.

"Has your well gone dry too?" I asked as I helped him load the barrels.

"No," he said, "the water has just sunk deeper in the ground, and I haven't time to dig it deeper now."

That fall when I had come back from the Chicago market with the proceeds of famine in my pocket, I met him under the bank clock.

"How are you wintering, Eric?" I asked.

"Pretty good," he answered. "I got rid of all my old ewes and I'm wintering twenty-five head of young ones. They're looking damned good."

The next summer he had a whale of a crop of oats and I went over with a team to help him thresh.

"How's the rheumatism these days?" I asked.

"Pretty good," he replied. "I went to that nose doctor in town and got my sinuses opened. It sure helped."

He limped over to his grain wagon, climbed in, and began scooping grain.

The next time he came to my place he was in great haste. It was sometime during the summer of '34. The dust had drifted his sheep fence under and his sheep had gone over the top of it into a neighbor's alfalfa field. He had run himself purple in the face trying to get them out and twelve of them were dead. I went home with him only to find that the others were so badly bloated that their stomachs stood high above the lines of their backs. We worked on them for two hours and saved them.

Eric examined the teeth of the dead ewes and said, "Well, some of them was getting kind of old."

A week later I heard a rattling sound coming down the road from behind the hill, then Eric's old Chevrolet coupe came in sight tugging behind it a big four-horse road blade.

"What are you going to do with *that*?" I asked him. "Move your place to a country where it sometimes rains?"

He smiled politely at my attempted jest and said, "I'm going to blade that dust away from my sheep fence. When it gets wet it's going to rot the wire, and I've got to have a good fence along that alfalfa field. I've hired a fellow with a tractor. I think we can blade it out of there in a day."

With that he set his machinery in motion and rattled on over the hill.

The Dust Bowl years were kinder to his rheumatism than the wet. He made a living somehow on chickens and milch goats and government soil payments.

It was in '39 that I saw him hobbling after those goats. He was no match for them, no match at all.

"Good God, Eric," I said. "Why don't you get one of those old age pensions?"

I thought he was going to hit me.

"Hunh!" he said. "Do you know what you've got to do to get one of those things? You've got to deed your land to the government. To hell with that noise."

I looked at his hundred and sixty acres of grasshoppered rockpile and thought privately, why not?

Aloud I said, "But can you handle those goats this winter, with your game leg and all?"

"Hunh!" he said. "I suppose you think I'm going to be a cripple all my life!" Then he told me about the new serum the doc was giving him, and how much better he felt.

When the rains came back Eric wasn't above rubbing it in. I had two miles of sheep wire that rotted under the dust, while his sheepwire was bright and tight.

I made a point of calling him on the phone because he looked like the wrath of God and I was afraid something would happen while he was there alone. But he was always all right and none too pleased with the implication that he might not be. I lost the habit of calling, and it was while my back was turned that the Devil made his final visit to Eric Smeel.

It was chore time in the morning and Eric had been aroused by his alarm clock. True to long habit his feet left the bed and sought the floor. But when he started for the stove to light the fire he found himself on the floor. His legs simply weren't there any more. He could see them, but he couldn't feel them at all. Then Eric looked up and saw the Devil. He saw the distance that cut him off from his fellow men. He saw the days that no one passed his place, and he heard the Devil say, "Do you surrender? Do you give up?"

Eric's eyes flicked past the Devil to the telephone screwed chin high to the wall and he said, "No, I won't give up."

Two days later I came in the door and found the house a wreck. Every article of furniture lay face downward on the floor. Everything that the hands of a crawling man could reach had been reached and toppled over onto the floor. The kitchen cabinet, the stove pipe, and an oil stove, all had come down. And there flat on his back in the pool of kerosene from the oil stove lay Eric Smeel.

I thought he was dead. Then he opened his eyes and said, "Hello, I've been trying to get you on the phone."

We took him to the hospital and I called there later that

day. Eric had come out of a coma of weakness and was talking a little out of one side of his mouth. He complained that his nightshirt was tight, and the nurse, knowing that it was the pain of the kerosene burn just beginning to get through to his mind, came with a hypodermic in anticipation of his pain.

At the sight of the familiar syringe, Eric's face twisted into a smile. "That doc!" he said. "Every time he gets hold of me he shoots me with that rheumatism stuff."

Two hours later he died, still thinking that he was alive.

It was quiet in the church, the minister had finished, the organ was still. I found that I was thinking about myself in terms of what had happened to Eric Smeel. His chores were dead and his house would fall apart and there would be nothing left of Eric Smeel.

But if his house were to stand for a thousand years, if bronze plaques and Centennial Festivals were to preserve intact the ritual of his chores, there would still be nothing in it all for Eric Smeel. Sparrows and eagles, once dead were equally dead. How did it profit an eagle to know what killed him, how did it profit him to have lived at all, if the whole race of eagles must surely die? Not even the Butte was immortal. Too bad that the sun would one day go out, and that the race of men must surely die.

250

Chapter XX

SUFFER THE LITTLE CHILDREN

NINETEEN years and one month after I returned from college to take up my Uncle's burdens I picked up the last one. It was a word — cancer.

I had heard it but my uncle had not. I had also seen the number of his room in the hospital, but he had not.

"What room is this?" he demanded suspiciously.

"Don't worry, it's not the same one." I lied.

"When are they going to operate?" he asked.

"Saturday," I replied.

He nodded and lit a cigar. "That's what I told the undertaker," he said placidly.

"You did what?" I yelped.

He was proud of himself. "I stopped in at the undertaker's on the way up here this morning. Told him to get a box ready because they were going to cut into me Saturday."

I couldn't cope with that one, so I let it go by. But he was always one to remember his own jokes and he remembered it on Saturday after the cart had brought him back.

"Well," he said, when the bottles and tubes had been taken away, and the needle had been removed from his arm, "I'm still here. Better stop in at the undertaker's and tell him I won't need that box for a while. How about a cigar?"

I saw that I had better keep the word cancer. And he was right, and I was right, though not in the way that he thought, nor in the way that I dreaded.

No one had convinced him that major surgery was not like a haircut, and that he shouldn't get up and trudge down the hall to the bathroom the first night. He did just that when I had gone home to the ranch.

The supervisor got hold of me by telephone and when I reached the hospital a little before dawn, he was in an oxygen tent and unconscious from every conceivable complication in the book.

It was by that route that I learned what a woman can do in a setting ten times more exacting than the kitchen on a ranch.

The crisis never slackened or stopped. As I stood in the door of Uncle Harry's room, keeping one wary eye upon him so that he wouldn't climb out of the oxygen tent to light a cigar and blow the place to kingdom come, the crisis went on around me. There were never more than four nurses and never less than fifty patients. There was never a doctor who had slept, nor a nurse who walked slowly. For the other nurses and doctors were in the Pacific, finishing the war with Japan.

SUFFER THE LITTLE CHILDREN

The lights over the doors, signals of pain and apprehension and discomfort, seemed always to be on. I heard a woman's voice moaning piteously, "Oh, I wish she would come, oh, I wish she would come." A man with a pale face and clad in a baker's uniform clotted with blood waited by the supervisor's desk with a badly mangled hand. The nurses were in surgery. The nurses were on Second Floor giving hypo's. There was a crash in a room down the hall and a man shouted hoarsely, "Nurse! Nurse! Goddammit, will somebody come and help this old fellow? He's fallen out of bed. . ."

Pain had to wait, though the nurses ran. To me, tethered to my own task, this crisis was a lambing in the mud, a roundup in a blizzard, a Battle of the Bulge, a Corregidor, and a Bataan.

But at seven in the evening, when the night supervisor came on duty, by some miracle pain no longer had to wait, and the woman's face, as it bobbed cheerfully up and down the halls, conceded nothing to the tide.

Once as she passed the door I said, "Shorty, I saw you go by with the surgery cart about ten this morning. Don't you ever sleep?"

She made a circle with her finger, held it lorgnette fashion to one eye, and clicking twice pertly with her tongue she said, "You should see me when I get the chance!"

My respect was profound.

On the evening that news of the Japanese surrender set the bells to ringing and raucous automobile horns clamored exultation in the street, I lay on a couch in a friend's home, trying to sleep, and seeing instead two hard alternatives on the wall before my eyes.

If Uncle Harry lived, much suffering for both of us lay ahead. If he died, then my life would lose a rudder that had given it direction for the nineteen years that I had spent upon our land. . . . .

I slept.

I was awakened by the ringing of the telephone. It was late — the automobile horns were silent in the streets outside.

"Hello," I said.

"Mr. Reeves?" Shorty's voice inquired.

"Yes."

"You'd better come."

I came.

But still it didn't happen. All day I peered in through the window of the oxygen tent to look at the face I had watched so long that every night I had gone to sleep feeling its drawn lines superimposed on my own face, like a mask.

Then it changed. The lines of pain left, and dignity came to take their place. The man who for a time had become my father, and then my son, became a father again, and his face knew more than mine.

A day or so later I came to town, fresh from the task of straightening out my neglected harvest, and intent upon completing funeral arrangements, I was stopped at Main Street by a "kiddie" parade. It was an annual event staged just before the schools opened their doors again, and for an hour it took over the business section of the town.

I joined the crowd in time to see a discordant and shambling "kiddie" band go by, followed by a long stream of the very young. The cement pavement was covered with forty or fifty wobbling tricycles, followed by a contingent of of bicycles, thence by a straggling clump of tramps and clowns and prospectors and cowboys with pearl-handled cap pistols. At the very end were the half-men on ponies who had ridden the tricycles five years ago.

In five years nothing in this parade had changed. Each year these self-proud faces pushed and pedaled and shambled and trotted up the street under the noonday sun, as though no tricycle had ever been pedaled before. Always before I had watched with the patronizing, indulgent smile expected of an adult who observes the antics of the young; but this year, because my perceptions had been so recently plowed and harrowed in the hospital halls, I saw something I had never seen before. I saw the Current that is bigger than the River, I saw the Hope that is longer than Death. Beyond the need for proof or reason, I knew that the tricycle would outlive the Butte.

I felt the need to share, and looking across the street I saw Shorty, with a coat thrown over her nurse's uniform, watching this endless thing walk up the street into Next Year. When our eyes met, I saw that we already shared it.

Here within the pages of this book are some of the things

a son of ours should know. This is the narrow plank on which I crossed a turbulent land. There may be broader, safer thoroughfares upstream and down, but this is the way I came, and if my soul is wrinkled, my feet are dry. When the time comes for you, my son, to recognize Death, think well upon this — you yourself would never have experienced the lovable and hateful light of day had any sparrow failed to fall at his appointed time.

AUTHOR'S NOTE

Some books can be written in a single, headlong flow of expression, and thereafter can be edited into readable and interesting literature. This is not such a book. Not only has it been revised from end to end many times, but it has been constantly exposed to the jostling of new experiences and enforced revisions of viewpoint.

It might appear that a book which has truth to lean upon could reach paper by a simple manipulation of a shutter in the author's mind and achieve its ends by simple photography. But truth is more elusive than that. In the writing of this book temptations have constantly arisen to deviate from memory in the interest of dramatic impact, and memory itself has not always been proof against the instinct to present matters in a more favorable light. Add to this the problem posed by the rights of living people, who might be humiliated or embarrassed by appearance in print, and one finds truth a difficult master.

In effect my task has been that of a pupil in mathematics who has the answer in the back of his book, but must reproduce step by step the phases by which it became true, and do it in terms of abstract x's and y's. The implacable sum in the back of this book has rejected passage after passage in which authorship attempted to improve upon truth; and the real, living people who were my neighbors had to be combined and abstracted into fictitious characters with fictitious names. In defense of this untruth in the midst of truth, the author can only assert that in no particular have these creations been permitted to dilute the validity of the known answer.

In presenting this material I wish to recognize the debt I owe to Professor R. W. Cowden, who for twenty-four years has nourished in me the belief that the expression of truth is worthy of labor and sacrifice.

Ann Arbor, 1950   GEORGE S. REEVES